Reflections

OTHER BOOKS AND BOOKS ON CASSETTE
BY ANITA STANSFIELD:

First Love and Forever

First Love, Second Chances

Now and Forever

By Love and Grace

Home for Christmas

A Promise of Forever

Return to Love

To Love Again

When Forever Comes

A Christmas Melody

For Love Alone

The Gable Faces East

Gables Against the Sky

The Three Gifts of Christmas

A Star in Winter

Towers of Brierley

Where the Heart Leads

When Hearts Meet

Someone to Hold

TALK ON CASSETTE

Find Your Gifts, Follow Your Dreams

Reflections

ANITA STANSFIELD

Covenant Communications, Inc.

Cover painting "Pewter Vase with Flowers" ©William Whitaker

Cover design copyrighted 2002 by Covenant Communications, Inc.

Published by Covenant Communications, Inc.
American Fork, Utah

Printed in the United States of America
First Printing: March 2002

08 07 06 05 04 03 02 01   10 9 8 7 6 5 4 3 2 1

ISBN 1-57734-993-8

Library of Congress Cataloging-in-Publication Data

*This book is dedicated to my sisters
in the Relief Society, worldwide.*

———— ✦ ————

*A special thank you to all of the many
people I've encountered in my life who have shared
their wisdom and insights in a way that
has left a deep impression on me.
It's not always possible to recall names and
faces enough to give credit where credit is due,
but the impact of our encounters is deeply ingrained in me.
Thank you.*

Introduction

———

We live in a world filled with diversity. As women in this world, we are no less diverse. We come from every possible walk of life, with experiences and personalities as varied as the markings in our fingerprints. No matter how many commonalities we may share, we are still unique individuals. Yet, in some ways we are all the same. No matter how our circumstances and personalities may vary, we all feel from a woman's heart and cry a woman's tears. As a gender, we are perhaps more in touch with our emotions, more in tune with the world around us, and more sensitive to how life affects us than men are.

We are all daughters of God, and His love for us is constant and intimate. But it's easy to lose sight of this simple truth in the midst of a world filled with confusion and deception. While we should be appreciating our differences and relishing our commonalities, we are often so caught up in just coping that we don't find the time or the inner motivation to do either.

In this day and age the world is often spinning so fast that it's difficult to get our bearings. Our lives can be harried and chaotic, whether we're struggling to raise children, working to keep the bills paid, meeting the challenges of a church calling, enduring a difficult trial, or perhaps all of the above. Through many seasons of our lives, we tend to be so busy that it's a challenge just to get in our daily scripture study and prayer. Yet we're told to ponder, to meditate. We're also told not to run faster than we have strength, although it often seems that running is the only way we'll stay on top of this spinning world.

A woman is like a well; if she gives and gives and never replenishes herself, she will eventually go dry. I have found this to be true time and time again, in my personal experiences and from the experiences of many, many women who have touched my life. But some of us are more stubborn about learning these lessons than others. Some of us have to go dry a few times before we realize how vitally important it is to keep drinking while we're trudging across the desert. I think I spent several years of my life waiting for someone to say, "You must be worn out, Anita. Why don't you take a break?" It was an epiphany for me to learn that it was up to me to take care of myself, so that I could be capable of taking care of those in my stewardship.

This book is about replenishing the water in the well—not in a way that adds one more thing to that already lengthy to-do list, but replenishing in a way that's feasible and workable, and well worth the effort. It has been my personal experience that finding even a little time every day to do something extra for myself can be difficult, if not impossible. But if I go too many days without doing so, I eventually end up unable to do anything productive at all. I have come to the conclusion that God gave us one day in seven to rest for various reasons, despite the fact that Sundays can have their own brand of chaos. But it's up to us to take the time to replenish ourselves.

So my challenge to you—and to myself—is to set aside at least one hour a week that's just for you. If your circumstances make that difficult, pray for a way to make it happen, and be creative. Perhaps you'll need to trade babysitting with someone else who needs the same opportunity. However you are able to work it out, make certain that you get the time to read something uplifting, ponder over your life in its present state, and consider your goals in relation to your life's direction. Decide if you're on the right path, or if you need to make some adjustments. Breathe deeply. Indulge in important and often neglected rituals of treating yourself like a daughter of God. And write in your journal; it's the pathway to clearing your head and sorting through your emotions.

My intent in writing this book is to offer the women of the world a handful of thoughts that might uplift and enrich, open minds and hearts, and give us something to think about. I'm writing from my own experiences as the mother of five and a writer of fiction. My personal struggles and insights may not be any more profound than those of any other woman, but I believe they illustrate typical patterns of opposition and trial that we can all relate to and learn from at some level. While many of the thoughts in this book are related to my experiences as a mother, my hope is that each thought I have to offer will contain a tidbit of value for every woman who might read it—old or young, married or single, with children or without. Whatever our differences in personality, opportunities, or challenges, we're all women. We all have tender hearts, strong spirits, and a desire to do the best we can with what we have to work with. We're all daughters of God, we're all trying to get to the same place, and we're all struggling in one way or another.

So, here's to seeking serenity. May we find it together. May we become better and stronger individually as we do so, and may we find strength and power as sisters united in a common cause to make the world a better place—and a little more serene.

Fleeting Moments

I've heard it said there is nothing in life as fulfilling—or as difficult—as motherhood. At this point in my parenting career, I'd say that's a fairly accurate description. Nothing in my life has ever been so completely challenging, but the joy I have found in motherhood is beyond description.

When my last baby was born, I felt a strong determination to enjoy every minute of the experience. It's not that I didn't enjoy my other children as infants; I was simply at a different season in my life, with a different perspective.

Looking back at the birth of my first two, both sons, I think I was so naive that I believed having children in my life would be nothing but fun and joy; I wasn't prepared for the full measure of how difficult and challenging motherhood can be. Although those years were filled with a great deal of personal growth, I still have countless tender memories of that time. John and Jake proved to be as different from each other as night and day (a cliché, I know, but it suits them well). Through the years it's been amazing to see such a stark contrast between their strengths and weaknesses. The two of them have taught me great lessons on how unique the human spirit is, and how love is never limited to commonality.

A five-year gap before the next child made me feel rejuvenated and terribly baby hungry. But life tends to be feast or famine. With my second two—a daughter and a son born fifteen months apart—I was so overwhelmed with the situation that it was difficult then to fully appreciate how precious the years of babyhood really are. I remember lying on the couch for most of that fourth pregnancy, watching my baby daughter and trying to absorb the memories through a fog, knowing that very soon she would be a big sister. And then they were babies together. Anna was small for her age, and Steven was a big baby. From the time he was two months old, they both wore the same size diapers. Now, at age eleven and twelve, they still wear the same size clothes and shoes. I call them twins of different pregnancies, because they really do seem like they should have been born together.

While having them so close together *was* a distinct challenge, especially because I get terribly ill with pregnancy and don't do childbirth well, I have often stopped to ponder how grateful I am to have them as close as they are. I treasure the pictures of them lying on the floor close together, drinking their bottles. I remember cleaning the highchair twelve times a day while they took turns eating their meals and snacks. And I've always cherished the way they played together so well—most of the time. There were those occasions (and we still have them) when they acted more like a cat and a dog. But they share a friendship that runs deep.

We knew that our family still wasn't complete, but it took us several years to get Alyssa. The pregnancy was not a surprise, and was joyously welcomed after so long a wait. But my own added years became quickly evident during the pregnancy, and I was continually grateful that my other children were old enough to care for themselves in many ways. In spite of being ill and down much of the time, I was determined to enjoy the experience. We knew this would be the last baby to come to our family. The completeness my husband and I both felt in our hearts was validated by increasing medical problems that made the prospect of my getting pregnant again almost suicidal. So, while I was enduring the many negative aspects of pregnancy, I made a conscious effort to absorb every *positive* aspect of the experience. I knew this would be the last time I'd feel a baby move inside of me, the last time I would feel the inexplicable connection of spirit to spirit as I prepared to bring a person into the world. I often felt a deep compassion for women who were unable to have this experience, while there were at least as many moments when I envied them for never having to endure the misery of more pregnancy-related health problems than I could count on my fingers.

Alyssa was born seven weeks early, after labor had been induced because of my high blood pressure. She spent sixteen days in the ICU, and came home weighing three ounces more than her birth weight of four and a half pounds. The many priesthood blessings given during the experience told us of the joy she would bring into this world—blessings that were quickly manifested. But those weeks of her infancy flew by so swiftly! Her little hands that were cast in porcelain by the ICU nurses are now much larger and capable of great destruction in the name of exploration and discovery.

Having more than a seventeen-year spread from the birth of the oldest to the birth of the youngest taught me to appreciate and enjoy those fleeting moments. I've learned that panicking over a fever or earache won't fix the problem any faster. I've learned to trust the Lord to guide me in solving those problems and in keeping my children safe and well; and I've discovered that my children could easily be older spirits than their parents, and I need to treat them with respect for their spiritual equality while guiding them with the temporal wisdom of my earthly years. I've also come to understand there is no deadline so pressing that I won't stop to hold my baby when the opportunity arises. And I've learned that love doesn't divide when you add a child to the family, it multiplies—not only toward the new child, but to the others as well. Alyssa's presence in our home has made me love my other children more. I feel more prone to stop my seventeen-year-old and wrap my arms around him, as if I can somehow hold the memories of *his* babyhood a little closer. I feel an added poignancy in the absence of my oldest son, who is on a mission, remembering the sweet relationship he shared with his baby sister, who will be so dramatically changed on his return. I find myself pausing more often to observe the play of Anna and Steven, knowing that these preteen years will soon be gone, and their childhood will have vanished with them.

There isn't a day that I don't feel crazy for chasing a toddler around at my age, even though I know many women have done it at a much older age. We've been told many times, "Oh, having a young one will keep you feeling young." I can see the point, but I more often feel very, very old. I had a lot more energy when John was this age. Still, the exhaustion is more than made up for by the snuggles and the laughter.

I marvel at what an incredible blessing motherhood can be, and while my heart aches for women who have been tormented by the lack of opportunity to have children in this life, there is great peace in knowing that, for those who live worthily, every hardship will be compensated for in the life to come. I have to believe that heaven must be a place where we can feel the joy of holding an infant close for the first time, and surely we will somehow be able to hold on to that joy forever. There is little that could be more heavenly than that.

The Tranquility of Morning

After recording the thoughts in the previous chapter, I recalled something I'd written down one morning. At the time, it felt good to record the moment, and now I would like to share the memory with you.

My first response to hearing my baby's cries breaking into my pleasant slumber is an inward groan. *Just one more hour,* I beg her silently, as if she could read my mind and suppress her hunger for the sake of my sleep. But a few minutes later, I'm holding her close to me in the bed while she draws on her bottle and tentatively explores my lips with her little fingers. The large second-story windows of the bedroom face east, and the light of dawn begins to filter over the mountains. A quick glance tells me it's a beautiful morning. Hints of pink lightly dust a few floating clouds that hover elusively over the snow-covered peaks, reminding me of the homemade quilt I'm snuggling beneath with my baby.

Now that I've torn myself from the lure of sleep, I'm actually grateful for the early-morning wake-up call. There's a certain tranquility at this time of day that can't be duplicated; it's like floating over a glassy lake, with the comforts of home close enough to touch, but not too close to intrude. Here is where embryos of great stories have appeared in my mind. Here is where solutions to the everyday struggles of life have been discovered. In this state—almost asleep, and not quite awake—I can feel my mind take on a new level of awareness, where the surrounding quiet serves as sweet fodder for inspiration. The glow of the sun and the song of birds is pleasant, but I know that beating rain or howling wind outside would not detract from such a moment. In fact, it might only contribute to my feeling of security in a warm bed.

As the baby finishes her bottle and turns wide eyes toward me, I fear the tranquility will be broken by her insatiable urge to explore her world. I know that within moments, she can have the same effect on the center of the bed as would the agitator of a washing machine as she struggles with zeal to find some avenue of uncharted territory. Her tenacity and determination are admirable traits that I often wish I could emulate in my middle age. But at this moment, my deepest hope is that she will allow me to continue this precious reverie for just a few minutes longer. I'm pleasantly surprised to look into her eyes and feel one of those rare soul-searching gazes that leads me to believe she has profound wisdom that would leave me in awe if she could only express it. She appears older in spirit than I am as she seems to grasp the tranquility surrounding us and allows it to take hold of her as well.

With a slowness that belies the nature of a nine-month-old baby, she turns her head to look at the room, as if she's never seen it before. Her perusal encourages me to notice that the rosy glow of the morning sun has changed the appearance of our familiar surroundings. *Alyssa Dawn,* I whisper, thinking that this is the kind of moment she was named for. She finally turns her gaze back to me and gives a tentative smile that seems to speak of the long talks and shopping sprees we will share in her adulthood, and at the same time, recalls vividly that, not so very long ago, we shared the same heartbeat. Her porcelain-white skin and wispy blonde hair give her the appearance of an angel. Hoping to keep her in this rare, ethereal state, I rub my hand gently over her tummy, clothed in soft, white cotton. She responds by humming softly, and within a few minutes, her eyelids are drooping. I am tempted to to give in to the urge to go back to sleep beside her, but there is a stronger desire to just watch her, amazed at how quickly she has changed from the premature infant whose foot was smaller than her father's thumb. Now, as she sleeps, her strength and resilience inspire me to make it through another hectic day.

I glance at the clock and realize I've got only a short while left before the other four children will be up and bustling noisily around the house. These moments are too precious to waste sleeping. After putting some water on to heat, I tiptoe through the children's rooms, finding the same sweet angelic evidence in their sleeping faces—even the teenagers'—that I'd seen in their baby sister.

Back in the kitchen, I quickly prepare a cup of hot chocolate before I slip quietly back into bed without disturbing the baby. While I sip my chocolate, I read a few passages of scripture and contemplate a message of peace, working it into my mental preparations for a day filled with the reality of motherhood and deadlines. But the dread of facing my mundane tasks is mitigated by the perfection of this moment, and by knowing that my life is filled with doing what I love. The room suddenly fills with bright light as the sun comes over the peaks. *This is happiness,* I whisper. Silence is all that answers me.

The Wash Cycles of Life

My mother once told me that in order to avoid feeling discouraged, I should try to accomplish one thing every day that won't have to be done again the following day. It's great advice, and I've genuinely tried to heed it. But in the midst of raising children, it can be easier said than done. The average homemaker could never count the hours she's spent sweeping and vacuuming floors that were swept and vacuumed the day before. The walls and windows can only be kept free of fingerprints and smudges for a matter of minutes. The toys only stay in their proper places for a serious length of time if you pick them up *after* the kids have gone to bed. The bathrooms will be inhabited by some grime-covered individual within moments after you've cleaned them. I could go on and on naming the repetitive, monotonous tasks that comprise a homemaker's daily job, but let me just conclude that the worst of them are laundry and dishes.

Imagine for a minute how many hours you might have spent standing in front of the kitchen sink. Can you tally all the laundry you've sorted, pretreated, washed, dried, folded, and hung or put away? It boggles the mind and tempts the most stouthearted woman to swoon. I think that one of the greatest things about heaven must be that it is clean and it stays clean. Can you comprehend the enormous amounts of time, effort, and money we all spend just trying to keep our world clean?

While dishes and laundry are different tasks, they have some startling similarities, the most annoying of which is the rapid reproduction process. As long as you only have one dirty dish in the sink, or one dirty piece of laundry in the hamper, everything's fine; you can rest easy. But the very moment a second one is added, reproduction begins with a speed and efficiency that puts rabbits to shame. Within minutes they will be doubling, tripling, and quadrupling their numbers, until the sinks and counters or hampers and floors are completely infested. As a result, even going a single day without tackling the problem will leave you submerged and defeated.

In fact, it takes great faith for me to not run the washer or dryer on Sunday. Gathering the laundry on Monday mornings can be a monumental task. Now, I really try to teach my children responsibility about such things. If their dirty clothes aren't in an appropriate laundry receptacle—which I have positioned in several convenient locations throughout the house—then I don't wash them. If they end up needing clothes that haven't been included in the normal wash cycles—because they've neglected to put them where they belong—they have to wash them on their own, or wait until I can get to them. This arrangement works fine until I think I've actually got the laundry caught up for the first time in four and a half months. Then a teenager will decide to clean his room, and I suddenly have a three-foot pile of dirty clothes to contend with. But since he put them in the hamper, I have little choice but to wash them.

I gave up folding my children's laundry a long time ago. They each have a basket in their rooms where I put their clean laundry. It's up to them to put the clothes away. It's amazing how many of those items end up back with the dirty clothes because they got thrown on the floor with everything else and the only way to tell if they're clean or dirty is to do the sniff test. My children are terrified of the sniff test. Body odor can be ugly.

I once reached a point, while I was serving as Young Women's president, that I knew if my kids didn't start doing dishes, they'd never get done again. Of course, when you're starting out with such chore training, it's easier to just do it yourself than to teach them to do it. But it's the principle of the thing. I refuse to have my children become adults without knowing how to wash a lousy batch of dishes. They were thrilled when we finally got a dishwasher, although I was amazed at how quickly after the arrival of the machine the condition of the kitchen deteriorated. It became evident that my children believed the dishwasher would also clear the table, wipe off the counters, and scour the roasting pan.

Eventually, with some persistence, my children really did learn to do dishes and even laundry rather well. It's amazing how capable they can be, once they find out they can't get away with pretending to be incapable. I'm a firm believer in the benefits of teaching children to work. My husband grew up on a farm, and he's often frustrated with the lack of work available for the kids to do. But with laundry, dishes, vacuuming, bathrooms, snow shoveling, and lawn mowing, we manage to keep them grumbling about the difficulties of life.

In spite of how much work you might assign to your children at the appropriate ages, the homemaker's work is never done. It's impossible for our children to comprehend all of the little things we do, day in and day out, to keep a household functioning and free of bacterial or fungal growth. And yes, it certainly can be drudgery. It definitely can be discouraging to do the same mundane tasks over and over, and never feel like you're getting ahead. But just as with much of life, perspective makes all the difference. My feelings toward the dishes and laundry were softened when I began to look at the jobs as service. When it comes right down to it, I wash dishes and do laundry because I love the people I'm doing it for. And I teach them to do their own dishes and laundry for the same reason. I want them to grow up to be capable, responsible, fulfilled, and consequently happy people. If I treat the drudgery of my housework as a discouraging burden, my children will grow up believing that being a homemaker is somehow demeaning and less than admirable. But if they understand that I do what I do out of love, it might actually inspire them to be a little more helpful, and a little less grumbly.

So the wash cycles of life go on, day after day, week after week. One day the kids will be grown and we'll be amazed at how easy it is to keep the dishes and laundry done. But once in a while we could visit one of our children—or someone else submerged in those child-rearing years—and we could do a big batch of dishes and a load of clothes, just for the fun of it. Maybe we can even pass along the wisdom we've learned through the seven trillion times we've done it before—that it's really not so bad. It's just a matter of perspective.

Cutting the Cord

I grew up in the Church. I saw my brother go on a mission. I married a returned missionary. Missionary work has always been in my life. It is a huge part of who and what we are; it's one of the points of the three-fold mission of the Church. And it saturates our culture. We talk of missions in past, present, and future tense. You can't stand in a group of Latter-day Saint men for long without having the question come up: *Where did you go on your mission?*

I always taught my sons (all three of them) that going on a mission was the best thing they could do with their lives. Their father and I always made it clear, however, that it had to be their choice. In spite of it being an admonition from a prophet of God, to go for the wrong reasons or against their will would be meaningless. The mission is something we've talked about, anticipated, and tried to prepare for. When my oldest son, John, was fifteen, we moved into our current ward, which had a lot of young people serving missions. We average fifteen in the field at a time. Missionaries are coming and going constantly. It is a challenge to fit the farewells and homecomings in around fast meetings and conferences. I'm constantly hearing mothers talk about the highs and lows of the mission experience. And always I've thought it would be hard, but oh so wonderful!

In the midst of preparing the paperwork for John, my brother (a returned missionary with two sons who have served missions) said to me, "It's like a freight train coming at you. It starts coming and there's nothing you can do about it."

As the papers went out and the anticipated call arrived, I felt the train beginning to roll. I often felt numb to the fact that my son would be absent from my life for two years; that our only contact would be through letters and two phone calls a year. There were moments when the reality seemed close and I shed a few tears. But most of the time we were too busy preparing to think about it. He would enter the MTC in the middle of January. The hustle and bustle of the holidays quickly merged into preparations that were far more overwhelming than I'd ever imagined. My sister marveled at the list I'd made of everything he still needed. I heard myself responding quite frankly, "Surprisingly enough, it's everything he needs for the next two years."

The reality really began to settle in when I watched my son walking out of Mr. Mac, pulling new suitcases and carrying a bag with ten white shirts, six ties, and two pairs of Doc Marten shoes. The tears started and weren't easily stopped. He was leaving me. His baby sister wouldn't be a baby when he came home. Life would go on and he wouldn't be here.

Of course I had every reason to believe he would come back. Some missionaries don't. It's a fact. But statistically speaking, they're still likely more safe on a mission than they would be doing anything else. The real problem for me was not only realizing how very much I would miss him, but to know that when he did come back it would never be the same. He would leave a boy and come home a man. (We hoped, at least.) It was like some tribal maturation ritual. And it *was* coming at me like a freight train.

Those final days were a harried frenzy. I kept thinking we should have been more organized, better prepared, but after we all got in the cars (we can never all get in one) to go to the MTC, I knew it had been better to be rushing around than to be sitting there staring at each other with time to think about what was happening.

Walking into the Missionary Training Center in Provo is an oxymoronic experience. The Spirit is strong. You feel good and positive and hopeful. You feel pride and pleasure as your child willingly joins the army of God, to spread truth and righteousness. Yet, all the while your heart is breaking. Will he be all right? Will he stay warm? Safe? Healthy? Will he be scared? Lonely? Homesick? Will he forget how much you love him? Did you teach him everything he needs to know in order to understand what he's up against? Being in the presence of dozens of other missionaries and their families and friends makes you feel understood, but a little lost in the crowd.

There is a crowd. The numbers are staggering. Having a deep conviction of missionary work, you can't help but be impressed by the number that enter the MTC every week. And there are other MTCs in the world. This one serves 9,000 meals a day, they tell us. They promise to feed our children well and see that they're cared for. We all sing *Called to Serve*, and then we say good-bye. The tears flow and you can't hug him long enough. Then he goes out one door, and you go out another. And that's when you feel it. Whether you literally gave birth to the child or not, walking out that door is the final cutting of the umbilical cord. Those final threads that you've clung to, despite of all your efforts to teach him to be independent and responsible, are severed with one harsh blow. There are volunteers in the hall holding boxes of tissue. I've never seen so many teary-eyed people in my life. I want to gather all the other weeping mothers in my arms and cry with them. But we all walk outside, glancing back over our shoulders as if we might get one last glimpse. I want to stop one of those tissue-carrying people and say, "Would you look out for my son? He's about nineteen, short haircut. He looks clean and fresh. He's wearing a white shirt and a dark suit."

On the way home, beyond an occasional sniffle, we have total silence. Even his sixteen-year-old brother is teary. I thought they couldn't stand each other. It feels as if we've just left a funeral. We're in shock. Dad admits later to being depressed. The ten-year-old brother gets upset at bedtime and can't calm down until his father gives him a blessing. Then we go downstairs to find out that the rumor is true: *Before the missionary goes to bed at the MTC, his little brother has overtaken his room.* He seems to have gotten over his sorrow. This morning John was in here gathering his things for final packing. This evening Jake is settled in comfortably. John's furniture is in the family room. Three days later his dad says he can't bear to take it apart and put it away. He says that going on a mission himself was never as difficult as sending a child.

When I realize there are over 60,000 missionaries out there, I wonder why one of the 120,000 parents couldn't have told me that I would feel this way. One woman admitted to my husband at the grocery store that the grief was like being in mourning. *Grief? Mourning?* Yeah, that's how I feel. But I can't help wondering over the grief parents might feel over having their son *not* serve a mission. Whether it's by choice, or whether some physical or emotional reason renders them incapable, that certainly must carry its own brand of sorrow.

That first Sunday after my son has gone, I sit in church and look around at the other missionary parents and wonder if it was this hard for them. When I ask, most of them admit that it was. But there seems to be a certain hesitance in admitting it, as if doing so might discourage others from going, or sending their children. I wonder if the glories and wonders of missionary service are among some of the myths we find in our culture, not unlike: *If you get married in the temple, you'll live happily ever after.* The thing is, it's not really a myth, it's just a theory that leaves out the middle part of the equation. You *can* live happily ever after if you get married in the temple. The middle part is that you have to live up to your covenants, work hard, communicate, and endure. And in that same respect, missionary work *is* glorious and wonderful. It brings great blessings to the missionaries, the people they serve, and the families who send them. But the blessings come through sacrifices. What does the song say? *Sacrifice brings forth the blessings of heaven.*[1] It's true, but the miracle comes *after* the trial of our faith. Joy comes in opposition to sorrow.

The bittersweet joy starts to trickle in with the letters John sends. The kids are suddenly eager to go get the mail. They gather around a letter as if it were a bag of Hershey's Kisses. We eagerly read as he tells us he loves his companion, he's made new friends, the food is great. Some letters are upbeat and some express more discouragement. He admits to finding it hard; feeling a bit home-sick and afraid. He humbly expresses his gratitude for all we've done for him. And then the words come that fill a mother's heart with incomparable joy: He knows that it's true. He knows that it's right. And you know that the conviction behind those words will get him through. That's the same conviction that will get *us* through, as well. It's the reason we taught them from their youth to serve missions, the reason it's such a huge part of the gospel *and* the culture. It's about sharing the light of Christ and spreading it throughout the world. And it is glorious and wonderful.

1. "Praise to the Man," William W. Phelps, *Hymns of The Church of Jesus Christ of Latter-day Saints,* no. 27, 1985.

Fievel Goes East

⎯⎯⎯⎯⎯⎯⎯

About the time we were getting ready to send in my son's mission papers, I was drying my hair on a Sunday morning and started imagining how it would feel to speak at his mission farewell. I laughed as an idea appeared in my mind, seemingly out of nowhere. I recalled an incident about John when he was four that I had always thought was so sweet. I could tell that story at the farewell, embarrass my son, and get a good laugh from the congregation. Of course, I understand that the farewell is a Sacrament Meeting. It is supposed to be an occasion for presenting gospel messages, not a forum for paying tribute to (or embarrassing) the missionary. But as my thoughts continued rolling, one thing led to another, and while I was standing there in the bathroom (now with a curling iron), I felt the Spirit teach me something completely unexpected. And I knew that I had to tell that story in my talk, because I had to share what I had learned. So, now that I've got you in suspense (it's a writer thing), I'm going to share my farewell talk with you. And you know what? John didn't get embarrassed when I told the story. Oh, well. We can't have everything.

When John was about four years old, we took him to see the animated movie *An American Tail*. I haven't seen it since, but as far as I can recall, it's the story of a family of Russian mice, immigrating to America to get away from the Cossack cats. Somewhere along the journey, Fievel, (the little boy mouse) gets separated from his father, and he's all by himself. At this point in the movie, John began to sob uncontrollably. He climbed up on his father's lap, and said over and over, "I know he'll never find his dad. I just know it."

We assured John that if he watched the movie until the end, Fievel would probably find his dad, and everything would be all right. He wasn't convinced, but he stuck it out. At the end, he cried just as hard, saying, "He found his dad. I'm so happy. He found his dad."

Well, that was the first time I realized what a sensitive heart John has. In the years since then, I've seen his tender concern for the feelings of others. I've seen his strong conscience and desire to do what's right. I never had to worry about him getting into trouble or doing something wrong. At a particularly difficult time, his father gave him a priesthood blessing, in which he was told repeatedly that he has a huge heart. I already knew that.

I thought of the premise of this children's movie, and how it applies to the life we live. It's about a child on a journey, separated from his father. And it occurred to me that a mission is somehow a microcosm of life in that respect. While a mission's main purpose is to spread the gospel throughout the earth, it stands to reason that sending a child on a mission gives us some level of sympathy for how our Heavenly Parents felt in sending us to earth, a place of so much uncertainty.

Pondering my son's departure into the mission field, I've often thought of what a fine missionary he will make with his huge, sensitive heart. Recently, while I was contemplating his tears on Fievel's behalf, I thought of the theme song from the movie. The words rolled through my mind and I shed a few tears to think of my son being someplace far away. *Somewhere out there, beneath the pale moonlight, someone's thinking of me, and loving me tonight . . . And when the night wind starts to sing a lonesome lullaby, it helps to think we're sleeping underneath the same big sky.*[1]

In the midst of contemplating how much I would miss my son, and how very difficult it would be to let him go, a different line from the song came to my mind with a certain impact. *Somewhere out there, someone's saying a prayer, that we'll find one another, in that big somewhere out there.*[2] And the warmth of the Spirit confirmed what I knew beyond any doubt. Somewhere out there, someone was lost. There was at least one particular someone who was trying to live a good life, trying to find the answers, and not understanding why there was something missing. And my son, *my son,* was the young man destined to be able to touch that particular someone with his sensitive heart and his testimony of

Christ. And suddenly it was easier to think of letting him go. Being without him for two years seems such an insignificant price to pay when you contemplate the difference he can potentially make . . . *somewhere out there.*

1. "Somewhere Out There," *An American Tail,* Motion Picture Soundtrack, Cynthia Weil, 1986.
2. ibid.

Sisters—
Friendship with a Silver Lining

The Saturday before Mother's Day, my sisters and I have a tradition of meeting for lunch with all of our daughters and grand-daughters. It's an occasion that we know must leave our mother smiling down upon us.

There is nothing in the world like a sister. I have a friend who only has brothers, and I feel truly sorry for her. She's been able to find friendships in her adult life that have greatly compensated for her lack of literal sisters. And, of course, we have to appreciate the family we were born into and make the most of it. But I am grateful to have sisters.

Because I'm the youngest by a span of several years, my sisters are both much older than I. (But don't tell them I told you.) I was five when one of them married, and ten when the other one did. But I was blessed to have one of my sisters living in the same neighborhood. We discovered a friendship as I spent a great deal of time in her home. One of them had moved away, but when she came back I was the number-one babysitter for both of my sisters' children. The real closeness in our relationships came, however, after I had children of my own. Once you enter the ranks of moth-erhood, it seems that difference in ages become irrelevant.

It was difficult when one of my sisters moved a few hours away, but it turned out to be a blessing in disguise when I was able to make a couple of trips a year with my children to stay with her. There's a closeness that comes from "staying" together that you don't get from occasionally going out to lunch—late nights of watching movies we loved, cooking together (unless we could avoid it), and most impor-tantly, laughing over things that no one else would think were funny. There seems to be an innate understanding between sisters that makes it possible to discover connections in the simplest of things.

Of course, the three of us are all very different as well. I believe that some of our greatest growth has come in learning to accept that we have stark differences, and it's okay. I've seen many sisters with frustrated relationships. The mere fact of being sisters leads you to expect each other to be so alike that you have difficulty understanding differences of opinion, or different ways of doing things. Celebrating our differences as sisters and allowing those differences to strengthen us has a way of further enhancing all that we have in common.

No one but my sisters would ever understand all the private jokes we've shared, and why they're so funny. And the fun we have when we get together is made richer by knowing that we can be there for each other in times of crisis.

Life somehow manages to get more and more complicated, and finding time to just be together as sisters often seems tantamount to climbing Kilimanjaro. It takes a conscious effort to nurture relationships that are of value to us, but it's effort well spent. One tradition that helps us maintain our unity is the Sister Christmas Party. It started out as simply getting together to exchange our Christmas gifts for each other when the extended family had become so large that we'd stopped doing a family gift exchange. Eventually we added some food, a good movie, and a discussion of our goals for the coming year. Now, instead of exchanging just one gift, we buy each other a number of little things we've collected through the year. We're always on the lookout for inexpensive items that remind us of the good times we've shared, our dreams for the future, or for something that will encourage some self-pampering. We quickly learned that the best time to hold the S.C.P was between Christmas and New Year's Eve. With all of the Christmas celebrations past, along with the stress, it's easier to relax and enjoy an evening together without children or phone calls to interrupt our precious time.

I could spend pages and pages recording the fun and laughter I've had with my sisters, as well as the sorrow and tears we've shared. But that's one of the greatest things about having a sister. No one but my sisters could fully understand the grief of losing my mother to cancer, and the care and concern for my father in her absence. Only my sisters shared the same struggles and cycles of being raised in our home by our parents with the influence of our ancestors. Sure, I've got brothers, and I love them dearly. I'm truly grateful for them and the relationships we share. However, it's just a fact that men see the world through different eyes than women do, and I'm so grateful that during the many times of sorrow and joy my sisters have been at my side.

Being with a sister can put a silver lining into nearly every cloud. When our mother was in the hospital with some serious, even life-threatening difficulties, I never would have imagined we could make positive memories. But we did. I have to admit that I became closer to my brothers through this time as well. For the first time ever, the five of us as adults were spending time together, without spouses or children around. Of course, there were many serious decisions to be made, and many long vigils in hospital halls and lobbies. But there were also many times that we got something to eat together following one of those vigils. There were times (thanks to patient nurses) that we all sat in our mother's ICU room until nearly midnight, talking and laughing. Our mother was at a point where laughter and distraction was a good thing.

Still, the best times through those several weeks of late hospital nights were with my sisters. We usually tried to be respectful of hospital policy and particular situations, but we learned that the staff, as well as the patients, could often use a little laughter and distraction. One particular evening, our father pretended not to know us as we borrowed a wheelchair (I had a sore big toe resulting from my own clumsiness) and my sisters pushed me around the entire hospital.

My sisters and I fixed up our mother's room with autumn decor when she couldn't get to the window to see her favorite season. We watched movies together gathered around our mother's bed, and we hung up every card she received through her long stay. Looking back, the reality of what our mother was going through is listed at the top of hard times in our lives. Many times we believed she'd never leave the hospital alive, or even if she did, we feared she'd never be able to eat normally again. But not so many months later, my mother and sisters and I all went to see *Little Women* at a theater, and a few months after that, we all went out for Chinese food together. Somehow, the memories of her hospital stay are more good than bad. For that, and for at least a billion other reasons, I am forever grateful for my sisters.

Tributes to the Guilt-Ridden

———————

I hate Mother's Day. Or at least I used to. Amazingly enough, I've found that those sentiments toward the holiday are far from unusual. I can't count how many times I've heard mothers say firmly, and with bitterness, "I hate Mother's Day!" For those of you who don't, congratulations. But read this anyway; it might give you some empathy for the rest of us.

Ironic, isn't it? A holiday set aside to revere and honor the greatest profession of womanhood has become—for many—a day that seems to do little but burden us with guilt and feelings of inadequacy. In my opinion, this enigma smacks of Satan's signature. Turning something good into something negative and distasteful is what he does best.

It's not difficult to understand why Mother's Day would be difficult for women who have been unable to have children. And women who have never had the opportunity to marry would certainly find Mother's Day difficult. I've appreciated being in a ward where the Mother's Day tribute is widened to include all women. We certainly don't mother our children alone. How could we ever do it without the Primary teachers, the youth leaders, and the Relief Society sisters who support us in countless ways? It truly does take a village to raise a child, and motherhood is much more far-reaching than the ability and/or opportunity to give birth. I would hope that those of us who have been blessed with such opportunities would be compassionate and sensitive to those who have not. Not in a way that draws attention to a difficult situation, or makes the single and childless feel pitied, but through quiet concern that is prompted by the Holy Ghost to touch a heart and lift a spirit.

Beyond the obvious difficulty of Mother's Day for women who have been denied those opportunities, why is it such a disagreeable holiday for many mothers in general? Start asking around and you'll quickly find a fairly unanimous answer: *guilt.*

While we listen to talks about how wonderful mothers *should* be, or the fine points of a few particular mothers in the ward (according to their husbands and children) our response tends to be a silent, mental calculation of all our faults in comparison. I will address this issue a little further on. For now, let's just say we shouldn't be comparing our Tuesday worst to someone else's Sunday best. It's important to remember that all the good qualities we might be hearing about one mother or another don't suddenly make that particular woman perfect. Forgive the comparison, but Mother's Day Sacrament Meeting talks are a bit like a funeral. We only talk about the good stuff, because it would be disrespectful—and inappropriate—to discuss the negative. Imagine a child saying over the pulpit on Mother's Day, "My mom's really great, even though she's a little overweight, gets angry occasionally, and doesn't keep a perfect house." Of course, it's unlikely to happen. But it's likely very true. So, before you start making comparisons, remember this: We all have strengths and weaknesses, and we'd do well to give ourselves an occasional pat on the back for what we're good at.

My son was once asked to give a talk on Mother's Day. I didn't know about it until late Saturday, when I heard, "Oh, by the way, Mom, I'm supposed to talk about you in church tomorrow." I had several people stop me afterward and say, "Your son gave such a fine talk." It actually did turn out very well, but I'm not about to lie.

"Thanks," I replied. "I wrote it for him." That's one way to get the right message across on Mother's Day.

Beyond that, it wouldn't hurt to point out to yourself occasionally what should be obvious. Motherhood in and of itself deserves some reverence and honor. I once had a woman say to me, referring to her mother-in-law, "Any woman who has burped that many babies deserves a medal." Of course, we can read between the words. Not just burped, but diapered, fed, attended through illness, listened to, put up with, taught, loved, and nurtured. Motherhood is full of ups and downs, and it's a learning experience for the mothers as much as for the children.

I've often found myself thinking of what a "bad" mother I am, as I focus on the times I've lost my temper, or handled a situation in a less than admirable way. But I've learned through the years that God forgives me for my motherly mistakes, and amazingly enough, the kids forgive me, too. I've learned that it's okay to admit to my children that I'm not perfect and I don't have all the answers, but I am trying to do what I feel is best for them and they're going to have to live with it. I've found that giving my children unconditional love makes up for a great deal. And I have to give myself credit for being a mother who genuinely wants to do what's best for her children.

So, if Mother's Day is something you're having trouble with, make a list of the good things you do for your kids, even if it's as simple as: *I keep them fed, and safe, and frequently hugged.* Then sit back, put your feet up, and tell them you're not cooking today. It's Mother's Day, and you've earned a few hours off.

Cats and Oil Paints

———∞∞∞———

Soon after my daughter, Anna, got a new kitten, my mother came for a visit. Watching Anna play with her kitty, my mother told me how much she'd always loved cats. I already knew that. But she also told me how she recalled, as a little girl, calling for her mother to come and see something cute the kitty was doing, or how sweet it looked lying in the sun. Her comment stayed with me as I watched my daughter regularly playing with her kitty, and how she would often call my attention to something the cat was doing. Thinking it through, I realized that I had done the same thing as a child. I'd always loved cats, and had played with them a great deal in my childhood. I guess we're just cat people.

But the idea struck me deeply on the Thanksgiving prior to my mother's death. I knew she likely wouldn't make it to another holiday season. She sat in the rocking chair in my kitchen. Anna put her cat on my mother's lap. She sat there contentedly stroking the cat's fur and listening to it purr. While Anna and my mother discussed the cat's beauty and personality, it struck me how very much my daughter is like her grandmother. I wondered how many generations of women prior to my mother had loved cats, and how many of Anna's descendants would feel the same way.

Since my mother passed away, Anna often reminds me of her. They're both just a little slow at catching the humor in a joke, and they both have a guileless kind of innocence that's difficult to describe. Anna also shares my mother's ability to find beauty in simple things. "Oh, look at that incredible rainbow," Anna will say. Or, "Did you see the way the sun was coming through that cloud?" She sounds so much like my mother.

In many ways, I think my daughter is more like my mother than I am. However, I've found it interesting to see how I might respond to something the way my mother would, or the ways I've purposely tried to emulate my mother. At one point, after her death, I undertook a personal challenge to make gravy that tasted the way hers did. Most specifically, I remembered when she would cook a roast in the oven, how heavenly the gravy would be. Memories of that gravy were warm and pleasant, and I wanted desperately to recreate the experience through my own cooking. I experimented each time I had the opportunity to cook a roast. I managed to make some great tasting gravy most of the time, but it just didn't taste like my mother's. I wished that she were here so I could ask her what she'd done.

One afternoon, while helping my father clean out some cupboards in his kitchen, I pulled out an old roasting pan. I had a picture of me as a baby sitting in that pan, which made me suddenly want to have it, for some strange sentimental reason. My father gladly let me take it, since he'd pretty much quit cooking. The next time I had a roast to cook, I used that old roasting pan. I was stunned to realize that I'd made gravy that tasted exactly the way my mother had made it. There hadn't been some great secret she'd taken to the grave. It was the pan she'd used. The very idea made me wonder how many things are inadvertently passed on from mother to daughter without any conscious realization, and how many things we try to emulate without understanding.

My second daughter, Alyssa Dawn, was born after my mother's death. Her second name was given in honor of my mother. While she was in ICU as an infant, and I was too sick at home to be with her, I felt comfort in thinking that my mother was looking out for her. I've discovered a different connection as I realized that my mother was the youngest in her family, as I am, and as Alyssa is. I look forward to seeing Alyssa's personality emerge, and seeing whether she might carry any characteristics of her grandmother.

As Anna has grown, I've noticed something else significant in her that completely skipped *me*. My daughter has amazing artistic abilities. My mother did oil painting, and her mother was an incredible artist. I can't draw a stick figure. Okay, I know I'm a writer. I have my gift, and I'm grateful for it. However, because I'm so lacking in drawing and painting, the ability to do it leaves me in awe.

Last year Anna became obsessed with oil painting. She begged me to buy her some oils. I was concerned, knowing how messy they can be for a child who has no experience. And I certainly couldn't teach her. Art lessons weren't feasible, but we did find out she could use acrylics to learn with and work up to oils. I realized how serious she was when she said earnestly, "Mom, I just know I can paint. I can see it in my head all the time." I told her that I could see stories in my head, so maybe I knew how she felt. And we went together to buy her some paints. Within hours of getting them home, she had done four paintings that actually took my breath away. For the amount of time she'd put into them, she had created images with concepts that showed incredible potential.

At some point when Anna was asking for paints, I recalled the painting classes my mother had taken during my teen years. I pulled her painting box out from beneath her bed and reverently touched the partially used tubes of oils, the brushes, the pallet she'd used to mix her colors. I talked to my father about them. While he had other grandchildren with artistic abilities, they were older and more well established. I told him it would mean a lot to me to have my mother's painting supplies for Anna. He agreed, and Anna was thrilled. I told her that after she'd done some serious practicing with the acrylics, and had gotten a little older, she could use her grandmother's paints and brushes.

They say that artistic talents can be inherited, but to see the mother I love immortalized in some small way through my daughter is something that fills me with joy beyond description. One day, we will all meet again beyond the veil and share in the joy our gifts have given to others. In the meantime, I'm enjoying the opportunity to watch my daughters grow, knowing that my mother is doing the same.

Angels with a Cause

I have learned to recognize what I call *Relief Society Moments*. Sometimes they have a great impact on us, and the memory stays with us through a lifetime. Sometimes they brighten a day, or even an hour, and the specifics of the situation pass from our minds with time. But we are always affected, and the effect stays with us eternally, whether in our conscious minds or in the line-upon-line development of our spirits.

I had one such moment when I answered the phone on a particularly "down" day. A woman I had never met was calling to tell me how much one of my books had helped her through a difficult time. Our conversation was brief. She was polite and didn't want to impose. But the way she brightened my day and lifted me is something that has stayed with me. She had made it clear that I'd been able to lift and help her. That's a Relief Society Moment—two women, touching in spirit for a moment to answer each other's prayers. Sometimes they're friends, sometimes vaguely acquainted, and sometimes strangers. That's what the Relief Society is all about. The casseroles and the babysitting are just a means to an end, and the end is charity—the pure love of Christ. As Christian women, it's our moral obligation to pass that love around freely. We start by giving it to ourselves, not in selfishness and indulgent gratification, but in having the self-respect of a daughter of God that allows us to be strong, confident, and firm in our beliefs. And then we reach out to our marriages, our families, our Church callings, our careers, our neighbors—whoever and wherever they may be.

During the ordeal of my last pregnancy, my family received approximately sixty meals from the Relief Society. Often they came in disposable dishes, left on my counter while I was upstairs in bed. Many times I didn't know who had brought the food, and some sisters brought food two or three times. The meals were wonderful. To know that my family would have a decent meal provided when I was so ill was truly a blessing. But that's not the heart of the blessing. It was the love that came with each salad, dessert, or main dish. The discouragement I felt through a very difficult time was lessened a little each time food was brought to the door. It was like getting a hug from my Heavenly Father, delivered by a woman who was oblivious to the fact that she was acting as an angel.

One afternoon when a friend was visiting, a woman in my ward came by with a pie. She told my friend, "Every time the sign-up sheets for meals get around to me, they're already full. I wanted to help, so I brought a pie." There's no describing the warmth of knowing that I'm surrounded by people who give so willingly. When the opportunity comes for me to put my name on that sign-up sheet and help someone else through their difficulties, I eagerly do what I can. It really takes so little effort to be an angel. And the cycles go round and round.

Growing up in the Church as I did, I spent some years with the misconception that service had to be a *project,* or something assigned by the compassionate service leader. I've found that some of the greatest opportunities to serve come through the quiet whisperings of the Spirit. Responding to a challenge from a Relief Society lesson, I began to pray for opportunities to serve that were within my means. I had very little time and no extra money, but I marveled at how the opportunities came. A neighbor needed a ride to the hospital to be with her baby who had pneumonia. It was the first time in weeks that my husband had been home with my two babies in the afternoon; so I had a vehicle and a babysitter.

Another time I was hit with a sudden bout of writer's block. The inspiration just quit. I thought I might as well go to the grocery store, even though I never went to the store at that time of day. While checking out my groceries, I noticed the missionaries one aisle over. They had a case of macaroni and cheese, a case of Ramen noodles, and many other essentials. I was well acquainted with the elders. I'd seen them at church many times, and they had enjoyed teasing my children. (One of them was from Australia—I loved to listen to him talk.) Taking note of their groceries, I recalled seeing their bicycles outside the store. I asked, "How are you guys going to get that stuff home?" One of them promptly replied, "Oh, we figured something would come up." It only took me ten minutes to load their groceries into my van and deposit them on the doorstep of their apartment. But the rest of my day felt just a little brighter.

One of the most effective means for charity to get passed around is through visiting teaching. I am deeply grateful for the many friendships I have found in my life that would not have come together if not for a visiting teaching assignment. Once again, the assignments are only the means to the end. It's not about the numbers; the numbers are just a way of keeping track of every sheep in the flock. When we take our assigned visits as an opportunity to enrich our lives, the entire perspective changes. When we make our visits with the intent to genuinely create friendships, we allow ourselves to become the conduit for the Spirit to answer prayers.

After my partner and I had been visiting an inactive sister for a couple of years, she confessed she was going through a deeply personal and traumatic ordeal. I felt my testimony of the visiting teaching program deepen as it quickly became evident that my partner and I could handle the situation because we had developed a genuine friendship with this woman that let her know she could trust us, and that we would listen and not judge. We were the right women to be able to understand and support her through many months of difficulty. I know we were not assigned as her visiting teachers by accident, and the friendship developed there went on long beyond the change of districts. This particular woman was the one who called me nearly every day to see if I needed anything when my husband was down with a back injury.

I wouldn't be where I am today if it weren't for the countless women of the Relief Society who have blessed and touched my life. I can't remember all the names and the faces; some were not active in the Church, but committed to loving their neighbors nevertheless. The simple acts of charity offered to me were not necessarily in bringing over a meal or helping me with a problem—although those things did happen. But there were countless little comments of support and encouragement, and things like letting my children come over to play at times when I needed a break most. The support I received from other women as I served in my Church callings made it possible for me to cope with everything else in my life.

The errand of angels is given to women.[1] How blessed we are to have opportunities before us every day to carry out those angelic errands, and to create those *Relief Society Moments.*

---

1. "As Sisters in Zion," *Hymns of The Church of Jesus Christ of Latter-day Saints,* no. 309.

Valentine's Day Isn't Necessarily a Bed of Roses

⸺◦◦◦⸺

Okay, before we go any further with this book, let's just get something straight. I'm continually amazed as I receive letters in response to my books, or as I travel around to speak at Enrichment meetings and similar functions. There seems to be some mistaken idea that because my name is foil embossed on the covers of all those beautiful romance novels, I must lead some kind of charmed life. Perhaps all of the inspiration for that romance comes from within the walls of my own home. So, let's just take a minute here and clear up the myths, because all this stuff I'm sharing with you in this book will be absolutely meaningless if you believe that I am somehow different from the average woman just struggling to get from one day to the next. Don't get me wrong. I have a good life. I have a great husband and great kids. I am extremely blessed. However, life is just *life* at my house.

First of all, allow me to take you on a virtual tour of my house. You're going to have to use your imagination, but try to focus. We're getting out of a car in the driveway. From here you can see a bunch of toys my kids never play with anymore piled up in front of the garage along with some miscellaneous junk, and up against the west fence there's the garbage that blew out of the garbage can a couple of weeks ago. Going up the walk to the porch, you'll notice that the flower bed here is severely neglected. No matter what season of the year it might be, it generally looks pretty sad. Not horrible, just sad. Whatever *does* look good in the yard should be credited to my husband, and the kids, provided he keeps after them to do their share. Okay, we're at the front door. Did you notice how long it's been since the porch was swept?

Inside the door, you'll see that the furniture doesn't really match the carpet. I got the furniture reupholstered just before we moved in, and it's never matched. Oh, well. I'm especially proud of all the marks on the walls going up the stairs. There are even a few holes that no one will claim. But we'll go upstairs later. While I can usually manage to make the front room presentable, this is where Alyssa plays. (She's two.) An assortment of crumbs and scattered toys are standard. The couch sinks in the middle. There are always video tapes and CDs scattered over the entertainment center because nobody ever puts them away, and that is where we put everything we don't want the baby to eat. Great decor! However, on the walls, there is a picture of Christ, a couple of great family portraits, and a picture of the temple. Home sweet home. You won't, however, find roses blooming beneath our feet.

On to the kitchen. One area of the counter is for the food that should be in the cupboards, but won't fit because they're always too messy. And that extra table in the corner of the dining area is for all the junk that never gets put away. If I leave the extra table there, we can actually use the dining table to eat our meals. What a novel idea! If you open the fridge you'll notice that it could use a good scrubbing, and you will likely find at least one container with mold growing inside of it. The freezer is filled with all the leftovers I didn't want to throw away and waste. Usually after they've been in the freezer for a while, the guilt isn't so great and it is easier to throw them away. The mud room is behind the kitchen, and it lives up to its name well. Just opening the door is often a feat in strength and agility given the opposing mass of shoes, hats, coats, and toys on the floor.

Now, the bathroom isn't too bad. That's because I pay Cindy (my dear friend) to come and clean it once a week. That's a line I crossed when I started making money writing. I pay a friend to mop my floor and clean my bathrooms once a week. If it weren't for Cindy, we'd be wallowing in filth.

Okay, now the office. You've got to love this room. This is where I write all those great books that those of you who like fiction might have enjoyed. It's supposed to be *my* room. I'm supposed to be a *professional*. So, how do you explain the piles of mail on the floor belonging to the rest of the family? The school papers? The bills? The magazines? The extra stash of paper plates? Are you getting the idea here? I could go on and on. This room temporarily becomes the north pole for a number of weeks each year, and it's the way station for anything and everything I need to take care of that doesn't know where else to go.

The basement is especially frightening. I don't clean down here. Only people we really like are allowed down the stairs. I won't get into too many details, because it might make you nauseated. The boys' bedrooms are . . . well, they're boys' bedrooms. The storage room should have a hard hat requirement to enter, and the laundry room is . . . a laundry room, and we never completely find the floor. (We've already talked about laundry, if you'll recall.) This bathroom Cindy *doesn't* clean. This one is to teach my children how to clean a bathroom. Oh well.

Now, if we go upstairs from the front room, you'll find a permanent pile of clean towels. They don't often actually get to the linen closet. The girls' bedrooms are . . . well, they're the girls' bedrooms. And the master bedroom . . . I'm sorry. I really can't do this any longer. My point was to make you feel like you could relate to me. I'm afraid you're going to be so disgusted with me that you'll never read another book I write for as long as you live. The point is, that in spite of living with a great deal of dust and disorder, our home is functional, and there is no obvious bacteria or fungus growing.

Having made my point with this ridiculous house tour, let me tell you briefly about a day in my life that happened a few years back. Valentine's Day was approaching. I was about to have a new book released. Since I write romance novels, having a release near Valentine's Day is good marketing. I was gone late one evening doing a speaking engagement. I came home and went right to bed. I woke up confronted with catastrophic surroundings. It was evident the children hadn't done their chores, because the house was a disaster. It was also evident that they hadn't gone to bed on time, because three out of four of them missed the bus. While I was standing in the middle of my chaotic kitchen in my pajamas, fixing lunches and nagging the children to hurry, my phone rang. It was a local radio station asking me if they could interview me— live—over the radio. "Not until I take my kids to school," I told them. I could just imagine what they would do—live—with the commotion in the background. *Interview with famous romance novelist interrupted by children screaming over who spilled the Kool-Aid.* I promised to call them back when I returned, then, still wearing my pajamas, I took the children to school.

I should stop here and explain this pajama thing. That's one of the facts about working at home that can't be avoided. When you don't *have* to get dressed and make yourself look good, it's easy to avoid it altogether. I used to try and get dressed early in the day, until I realized that self-discipline wasn't one of my strong qualities, so I just started buying modest pajamas. My husband now buys me new pajamas every year for Christmas, and tells everyone they're work clothes. This last Christmas they were covered with little cows with big red lips and roses in their teeth, sitting on the moon. What do you suppose he's implying?

So, anyway, I took the kids to school in my pajamas, then came home and called the radio station. I'm listening to myself doing this live interview, imagining myself sitting on the Oprah show, looking absolutely stunning. But there I am, standing in a messy kitchen—in my pajamas. (The glories of radio.) When the interview was over, I got right to work at the computer. With a deadline looming, giving the house any extra attention was not an option. My publisher called to let me know there would be articles running in a couple of newspapers that day to promote the new book. When my son came home from high school, I sent him to get the papers because—yes, I admit it—I was still in my pajamas. He brought them home and I opened the first one to read, "Every day is Valentine's Day for Anita Stansfield."

I took a look at my surroundings, with myself in my pajamas sitting in the midst of them, and I got fairly depressed. Of course, when my husband came home, I was still in my pajamas. I'm usually showered and dressed at least before he gets home, but not *that* day. I told him I was not behind, I was ahead. But he knows me better than that. He looked at that newspaper article and he laughed. I mean he *really* laughed.

The Valentine's Day thing has gotten to be a joke around here. When the food is burning, the kids are screaming, and the house is a mess, someone will pop up and say, "It must be Valentine's Day." I didn't realize how well trained my children had become until one afternoon at Cub Scout Bear den meeting. I was the assistant leader, and my son, Steven, was in the den. We were talking about manners; good ones as opposed to bad ones. When an example of bad table manners came up, I said to Steven, "That sounds like our house, doesn't it?" Without blinking an eye or hinting at a smile, he said firmly, "No, it's always Valentine's Day at our house."

So, that's the truth of it. Being the mother of five, with a Church calling to hold together, and working more than full time (even though most of it's done at home), I simply don't have the time to be an immaculate housekeeper or make myself look picture perfect for anyone who might stop by. There was a time when I suffered an immense amount of guilt over this very issue. I believed that I had to be everything to everyone, and if I wasn't, there had to be something wrong with me. But through the guidance of the Spirit and some hard lessons learned, I've come to see that I am capable of accomplishing only so much in a day, and no one but me can put unreasonable expectations on me. If others are asking and expecting things from me that I'm not capable of giving, it's up to me to draw the line and put my priorities in order.

For me, in this season of my life, it's more important to be aware of my children's moods and make regular contact with them than it is to have the floor vacuumed or the closets organized. It's important that my children get fed, but they usually don't care if the meal took fifteen minutes or two hours to prepare, and there are days when it's all right for them to heat up leftovers or a hot dog on their own. If you ask your children which they would prefer—chicken cordon bleu and an ornery mother, or macaroni and cheese and a pleasant mother who is open and available to them—I wonder which they would choose.

I've thought a great deal about Mary and Martha, and choosing the better part. I've realized that the better part can change from day to day, or even hour to hour. Sometimes the better part is stopping everything just to hold the baby, because she wants to be held right now, and tomorrow—or even ten minutes from now—she won't. I try to look at a day—or even an hour—and tackle what's most important right now. By keeping church and family first, and trying to respect myself and what I'm capable of, life usually doesn't get too far out of balance. Of course, life is crazy and it's a constant challenge to keep that balance. And that's one of many reasons I'm so grateful for the gift of the Holy Ghost. I'm continually amazed at how willing my Father in Heaven is to guide me on what's important, by speaking to my thoughts and feelings through His Spirit. I may wake up and decide that today is a writing day. I have to get a lot done, and I'll only do the bare necessities otherwise. But if a friend, or family member, or a sister that I visit teach calls with a problem, I know in my heart where the priority has to be.

So, the conclusion is this: if you learn to accept that even Valentine's Day is just a day on the calendar where you might stop and pay a little more attention to the people you love, I guess the rumor is true. Every day *is* Valentine's Day. Or at least it should be.

Thoughts from a Hopeful Romantic

⸎

I'm well aware that I'm known as a romance novelist. I admit it. But I think I should clarify myself on that point. After writing romance novels for more than twenty years, I've picked up on a thing or two that has surprised me. My perception of romance when I began writing at the age of sixteen was much, much, *much* different than it is now in my middle age.

I've noticed that for some people, the very notion of *romance* seems to have a stigma. Naturally, there are many people who have suffered through divorce or equivalent challenges that make it difficult to believe in happy endings. In fact, I've been asked more than once, "Why do you always write happy endings? There is no such thing as a happy ending."

My response to that has been, "If you're standing there talking to me, it isn't over yet." The truth is, I'm well aware that real life can be tough—for some more than others. But I believe in happy endings. Books should have happy endings, if only to encourage us to hope for something better. As Latter-day Saints, we believe in enduring to the end, knowing that if we live righteously, we will return to live with our Father in Heaven. You can't get a happier ending than that.

The word *romance,* among other definitions, also refers to a genre or category of entertainment. And for many, this is where the stigma originates. Out in the world, the book industry makes big money in romance. But most *romance* novels are either fluffy and trite, or trashy and offensive—or both. Just as with many other things in this world, Satan has taken something good and turned it into something ugly.

I see romance as the feelings and experiences that bring a man and woman together, and keep them together, in spite of their personal struggles and outside conflicts. We have all been given an innate sense of attraction that leads us to want to be with someone, marry, have a family, and stick it out. There are all kinds of struggles that come into the picture. Nevertheless, defining "romance" in such a way makes it a very righteous and appropriate thing. I've always believed that people who enjoy reading fiction ought to have the opportunity to read something that not only entertains, but uplifts, enriches, and even teaches. But Satan has turned the romance genre into something evil and ugly, defiling and desecrating the God-given gifts that were intended to bless our lives and bring us joy in our relationships.

Because the word *romance* carries such a stigma for some people, I would prefer to have my work called *relationship fiction*. But that isn't a particularly good marketing term. It's a bit wordy on the posters and book covers. So, I have to accept it. I'm a romance novelist. I'm okay with that, but sometimes I have to take a few minutes to explain to the romance cynics that I'm not your *typical* romance novelist.

I've learned to distinguish very clearly the line between fiction and real life. That doesn't mean, however, that I'm not prone to becoming very emotionally involved in my work, and that my characters don't take on a certain reality for me. But I'm happy to say that I haven't become psychotic as a result. So allow me to define two very distinct categories of romance that actually have a great deal in common: fiction and real life.

Fiction is not real. That's the definition, in fact. It's a story. But that's not to say that my books don't have an edge of reality. I've always believed that the story has to touch real emotions and deal with real problems in order to have any impact on the reader. My plot lines and characters are not real. But many of the situations they encounter are based on bits and pieces of reality that I have observed in people's lives. With that in mind, let me tell you what romance means to me in terms of its place in fiction.

After writing for more than twenty years, and more than thirty novels (some are not in print yet), I've come to believe that real romance is the mutual love, respect, and admiration between two people. It's not riding a horse with the black-clad hero across the outback of Australia. (Although that *does* have some measure of appeal.) And it's not dancing in the dark to the same song over and over. (Even though that certainly has its high points, given the right partner.) It's not even flying in a prop plane with one of the country's wealthiest bachelors. (Which *could* be terribly fun, however.) In spite of the high romantic moments that I have interspersed in my stories, for the purpose of provoking a deep sigh from my readers, the real romance emerges when the characters illustrate commitment in the face of horrible circumstances. Romance shows itself when the hero speaks respectfully to the woman he loves, even when—or especially when—he's angry with her. Romance comes out in the examples of appropriate communication between two people as they work to overcome their challenges—together. Romance is best seen when people disagree, make each other angry, cause each other grief, and endure life's typical problems, yet still remain true and strong in their commitment to each other.

You must understand that I actually *agree* with people who say that romance novels aren't good for you. It's true—part of the time, at least. If a romance novel only shows an idealistic side of life without showing the reality at the same time, it can do a disservice to readers who are more prone to get lost in a book than face their own lives. But if a book can encourage the reader to buck up, face the music, take responsibility, and take action, then it has the potential to make a positive difference in lives and relationships. And LDS novels can enhance this effect when characters use gospel principles to solve their problems, and their testimonies are strengthened in the process. Personally, it thrills me to see so many good LDS authors continually expanding the number of books that fill these purposes.

Now that I've given you my editorial on romance novels, let's talk about real life. In truth, many of the same concepts apply. Sure, I love it when my husband comes home with flowers. He doesn't very often, which makes the occasion all the more thrilling. And I absolutely love the rare opportunity to get away with my husband for a nice dinner out, or a night at a bed-and-breakfast. But real life doesn't allow for such events very often, especially during the child-rearing years. However, real romance has a way of showing up in the most surprising places. For a frazzled mother, having your husband spontaneously offer to bathe the baby and put her to bed is extremely romantic. When pressed with a deadline and piles of laundry, I find it deliriously romantic to see my husband leave for The Home Depot with the baby in his arms and a baby bottle in the back pocket of his jeans. I feel loved and respected when he makes certain the children have done their chores and their homework. And there is almost nothing that is more romantic than having your *hero* step between you and the snarling teenager, to say firmly, but with love, "I'm not going to let you treat your mother that way. If you're going to act like that, you can deal with *me.*" How could I feel more loved than that?

And occasionally we have those *really* romantic moments when we spontaneously dance together in the middle of the kitchen. He's usually just come in wearing his work clothes, dusted with a day's construction, and I'm often (of course) in my pajamas. But such an event has a way of shutting out the surrounding chaos and saying clearly, "For a few minutes you're all mine, and I can just appreciate you and how much we've been through together." I love the romance of having him insist on sitting next to me in Sacrament meeting, instead of putting the kids between us.

You feel the true reality of romance when faced with difficulty or crisis. The ins and outs of everyday living are the true heart of romance. As I've said before, I don't live some exotic, charmed life. My life is simple—and real. My husband and I joke about having three things in common: our address, our children, and our religion. We used to have the same phone number, but now we have cell phones. Nevertheless, we've learned to accept our differences and make the most of them. We've learned that our shared commitment to our marriage and the raising of our children is more important than whether or not we both like the same movies. And the love we share in our marriage is made sweeter by knowing that it hasn't always been easy. By sticking it out and sticking together in spite of our differences and struggles, I have felt the love between us become far deeper and richer.

It's understandable that I would be called a romantic, but I must confess that the most romantic interchange I have ever observed took place between my parents. Although it was only a moment, you must understand all that led up to that moment. My mother had endured some years of illness, mostly related to cancer. I had watched my father sit through long vigils at her hospital bedside, and I had watched him lovingly see to her every need when she was at home in his care. He fed her through a stomach tube, and meticulously prepared her medications week after week. When it was finally almost over, I watched him sit for hours beside her bed in the room they had shared for decades. I thought of the years they had shared—fifty-three of them. They had married young and had endured a World War and many struggles in raising their five children. Now she was leaving, much sooner than any of us had expected. I knew his heart was breaking. I knew that being without her would be more painful than any of his children could comprehend. But he took her frail little hand into his, and spoke to her in gentle tones that she probably couldn't hear in her unconscious state. He told her that he knew she was tired, and she could leave now if she needed to. I can't fathom his courage in being willing to let her go peacefully. Nothing before or since has ever struck me in such a deeply romantic way.

I suppose now you can understand why people call me a hopeless romantic. But I prefer to be hope*ful*. I have every hope that my most romantic moment will be when my sweetheart and I are reunited on the other side of the veil, following the separation of one of us dying before the other.

So, there you have it. When I write books, I guarantee happy endings. And when it comes to real life, I can only say that I know there is a happy ending in store for each one of us, as we live worthy to receive those eternal blessings—whether we end up with a hero in this life or not.

Balancing the Scales

⌘

Looking back over my life, I could probably pin the majority of my personal struggles down to one main point: *inadequacy.* I've always struggled with my feelings of low self-worth and a lack of confidence. My parents are good people, and I deeply love and respect them. But they also struggled to feel good about themselves, and their inadvertent example left me feeling much the same way. I've studied many self-help books, had lengthy discussions with friends who have similar struggles, and I've prayed for day-to-day guidance to get past the feelings and behaviors that have made life more difficult for me and for those I love.

You might think that a woman with all those published books and related awards should feel pretty darn good about herself. But I had to overcome a certain degree of these negative feelings toward myself in order to achieve my goals, and it is something I continue to be challenged with. However, through the years that I have been consciously aware of this challenge, I've discovered something interesting. I have never had any kind of in-depth conversation with any woman of any age (and I've talked to a *lot* of women) without discovering in them some level of feeling inadequate. It seems to be an epidemic. I believe that's because we're so easily persuaded by the whisperings of temptation.

I'm not talking about being tempted with the big stuff. We women who are genuinely trying to do what's right, raise our kids well, do our Church jobs, and keep the bills paid, are not easily tempted with the big stuff. Satan doesn't start out by whispering, *Why don't you and your visiting teaching partner run off to Las Vegas and blow the house payment?* Or, *Why don't you and the Relief Society president sneak out and guzzle a six-pack of beer?* All levels of struggle exist among members of the Church, but the great liar knows better than to tempt us with something so easily identified as destructive. We don't give in to the big stuff, and he knows that. He starts out with the subtle whisperings to make us sit up and pay attention. He whispers things like, *You're the only woman in this ward who doesn't really measure up.* Or, *It's too bad you're the only woman on the street who doesn't have a perfectly organized home.* Or there's the all-powerful *What a shame you can't manage to be everything to everybody all the time.*

Satan knows just when to throw the punches during the emotional cycles that women are prone to. A little whisper goes a long way when we look at the flaws of our lives through a magnifying glass and everyone else's through a telescope turned backward. We compare ourselves with others—and we're all so good at it that you would think we'd been trained somewhere along the way. You look at yourself in the mirror on one of those really bad days: you need a shower, and a haircut wouldn't hurt. It's that time of the month, and you have a head cold, and you didn't sleep well. Everything around you is in disarray, and the pajamas you're wearing are something Deseret Industries might consider using for rags. While this image is so clear in your mind, you think of every woman in your ward and how they looked in Sacrament Meeting on Sunday. "Tuesday worst" on one side of the scale for you, and "Sunday best" on the other side of the scale for everyone else. Where's the fairness in that?

I'd like to share with you a theory on self-worth that a psychologist friend once shared with me. It's great having a psychologist friend in this business. He's not only helped me analyze the behavior of my characters as they've dealt with all kinds of challenges, but he's always willing to check my emotional barometer—which never hurts when your brain spends so much time in other people's heads (even if they're not real people). Anyway, I was once discussing with my psychologist friend the struggle I had with feeling good about myself, and he shared a theory with me that has made a huge difference in my life.

He said that we tend to base our value as a person on things going on around us. For instance, we subconsciously say, *I am a woman of value because I keep a perfectly immaculate home.* Or *I am a woman of value if I have a great career and make a lot of money.*

Or there's often the *I am a woman of value if I raise happy and righteous children.*

Now, the problem is, there comes a point where it's not possible for you to be in control of the circumstances any longer. What happens if you've kept a perfectly immaculate home for seventeen years, and then you get a chronic illness, or someone you love becomes ill? What if you have to go back to work and don't have the time to devote to your home any more? What happens to the way you feel about yourself? And what if you've spent your life working up the career ladder, only to have the bottom fall out of the company and you're suddenly unemployed and starting over, through no fault of your own? And what about raising happy and righteous children? Look at Lehi and Sariah. They did everything within their power and knowledge to teach their children correctly. But Laman and Lemuel were past feeling. So, what if you're blessed with a Laman? You have to understand that no amount of good parenting will change what a particular child will do with their free agency.

The point is that you cannot base your value as a person on circumstances beyond your control, or on the free agency of other people. Such beliefs will leave your self-worth walking a precarious tightrope, and it will inevitably fall. But there is a safety net that is fool-proof. There is only one place you can rest your value from where it will *never* fall. It is the absolute knowledge within yourself that you are a daughter of God and He loves you unconditionally. He is always there to carry you; always there to see you through.

Allow me to clear up a common point of confusion. We know that logical consequences result from committing sin or indulging in weaknesses. We also know that blessings are consequences of righteousness. But Satan would like us to believe that these blessings or unpleasant consequences are interrelated with our Heavenly Father's love, when in fact, there is no connection. The love He has for us is absolute and unconditional. It has nothing to do with our performance or behavior. Let me repeat that: His love for each and every one of us is absolute, constant, and unconditional!

I once went through an eight-week course for displaced and abused women as part of the research I did for a book on domestic violence. In the class, the teacher challenged the women to look at themselves in the mirror two or three times a day and say, "You are beautiful." She said that it would be extremely difficult at first for most of these women; they had been through horrible ordeals that had eaten away at their self-worth. But she promised that if they did this exercise diligently, they would begin to feel differently about themselves, and subsequently people would respond to them in a more positive way. She promised that if the changes didn't materialize, she would take them out to dinner. In ten years of teaching the class, she's never had to take anyone out to dinner.

I pondered taking the concept a step further. Why not look at ourselves in the mirror and say, "You are beautiful, and you are a daughter of your Heavenly Father, who loves you."

Sounds familiar, doesn't it? After working in the Young Women's program for many years, I have a deep testimony of the inspiration behind the theme that is repeated aloud at every meeting. I believe that our leaders were divinely inspired to teach and remind our young women who they are and of the love that is always there for them. I've been saying for years that we Relief Society women need a similar theme, and now we have one. If you don't have a copy, get one. Put it in a prominent place and read it often. See if it doesn't make a difference in how you feel about yourself.

The bottom line is simple, and I can't say it any better than this: *We are beloved spirit daughters of God.*

I Hate Play-Dough and It's Okay

Speaking of feeling inadequate . . . There was a time in my life when I was struggling—I was down about the areas where I seemed to be lacking in talent. For some reason those feelings were quite prevalent in my mind when the Relief Society president called. I had been expecting the news, but it was shocking nevertheless.

I had been assigned quite some time earlier to be a visiting teacher to a woman named Ellen. Through our visits we had become good friends. She had given me a great deal of validation and encouragement about my ongoing rejections while trying to sell a novel, and I had done my best to be compassionate to her—she had breast cancer, and the prognosis wasn't good. The phone call I got from the Relief Society president was to tell me that Ellen would be coming home from the hospital. There was nothing more that could be done. She would likely be in a hospital bed in her front room for what little was left of her life. They needed sisters to sit with her during the days while her husband was working, since her two youngest children were a preschooler and a kindergartner. She didn't want her children taken out of the home; she wanted to spend as much time with them as she could. So, the president was starting with Ellen's visiting teachers to see who might be willing to help. Apparently she'd already determined from casual comments that there were a number of women who were willing to watch children for others who would go into the home, but many were reluctant to go and sit with Ellen. I heard myself readily volunteering, "I'll take Tuesdays." But as soon as I hung up the phone, I felt prone to join the reluctant forces. What had I done? How could I spend several hours a week with a dying woman? What would I say? What if I started to cry? I posed these questions to my husband and his response was something to the effect that if I cried, that was fine. Maybe she needed to have someone to cry with.

So, I prayed for guidance and courage, and I showed up ready and willing Tuesday morning. I immediately asked her what I could do to help, and she asked if I could hem a pair of pants for her son. The irony here is that I *hate* to hem, and I'm not very good at it. I have used many levels of bribery to get my sisters and friends to do hemming for me, because I *hate* it. But I just smiled and said, "Sure, I'd love to."

While I worked to hem the pants, Ellen and I visited casually. As usual, she was bright and positive. She was an incredible example of facing her struggles with a positive outlook. But I sensed that something was troubling her. I asked her a number of times through the morning if something was wrong, if there was something bothering her that I could help with. She assured me that everything was fine. I helped with the children. I got her whatever she needed. We chatted about odd things and the weather, and I felt like I was handling the situation relatively well—except for that ongoing feeling that something wasn't right.

Early that afternoon, Kim, a mutual friend, popped her head in the door and said lightly to Ellen, "I heard you were sick and you didn't tell anybody." Now, that was a ridiculous notion, since Ellen was dying and *everyone* knew about it—so Ellen laughed. Following some casual conversation, Kim said, "Something's bothering you. What is it?"

Ellen immediately started to pour her heart out about some concerns with a prescription, and something she wanted to discuss with a doctor. Kim got right on the phone, called the right people, got the answers, and Ellen felt better. Now, I'm watching this scenario unfold with the question blaring through my mind: *What's wrong with me?* I wondered why Ellen hadn't felt comfortable enough with me to let me help in this area. I went home feeling extremely inadequate.

It was much later before I began to get the clear picture. It started when I was blessed with the opportunity to have Kim cry on my shoulder. (Not quite literally.) The details don't really matter. It boiled down to one thing: she was feeling extremely inadequate. After that day I began to take notice of Kim, who actually lived next door to me. I found she was an amazing woman. I finally summed up that some of her greatest qualities are the gifts of friendship and compassion. She's an extremely social woman, who makes a point of knowing everybody and what's going on in their lives. It doesn't matter if they're members of the Church or whether they're inactive; if they live within a certain radius of her home, Kim knows who they are. And she's not just casually acquainted; she has invested enough effort into getting to know these people that they call her to share good news or bad. And that's where the compassion part comes in. Kim has paid more visits to hospitals and the homes of ailing people than any five other people I know. She's gifted. It's as simple as that. Ironically, Kim had difficulty seeing her gift because she was more preoccupied with all the things she *wasn't* good at.

Now, let me tell you about Becky. When Becky moved into the neighborhood, my daughter, Anna, was thrilled. Anna was about four, and there was a severe shortage of little girls in the area. Becky had a daughter near Anna's age. Julie and Anna quickly became the best of friends. When Julie came to play at our house, I would usually say something like, "You know where to find me if you need me, but I want you to play and be quiet, because I'm writing. Okay? Thank you." *But . . .* when Anna came home from playing at Julie's house, her report would excitedly include at least one of the following: "We made roll-out cookies and decorated them with little sprinkles. We had a tea party with our dolls. We cut paper and used glue and glitter. We played with play-dough." That last one really bit. Play-dough was illegal at my house. I had dug it out of my carpet so many times that I couldn't take it any more. In fact, I had a good friend who loved to have Anna and Steven come over and play because she could sit them in front of play-dough and they'd be content for hours; they were play-dough deprived. I *hate* play-dough.

However, back to the point. Hearing of all the fun that Anna had at Julie's house began to make me feel like a really bad mother. I love my children. I really do. And I've always made it clear that they were my first priority, and I have always made a conscious effort to be aware of their emotions as well as their needs. But I'm just not into all these fun little projects. And to pour lemon juice on the paper cut of my inadequacy, Becky started teaching preschool in her home.

But then, I was blessed with the opportunity to have Becky cry on my shoulder. (Not quite literally.) The details don't really matter. It boiled down to one thing: she was feeling extremely inadequate. After hearing it from the mouths of two witnesses, I started to get the idea. Becky had a gift, just as Kim had a gift. She did well at relating to preschool-age children. She enjoyed doing things with them and for them. But she had other areas in her life that left her feeling down on herself and maybe even intimidated, because she wasn't so good at them. Ironically, some of the things that Kim and Becky struggled with were things that I could be really good at and feel confident doing.

That's when it finally started to sink in. Most of you probably figured this out at a much younger age than I did. But . . . well . . . *duh* . . . we all have strengths and weaknesses. And . . . *duh* . . . if we all had the same strengths and weaknesses, the world would be terribly lopsided. For me, personally, I'm really glad that everyone out there can't write stories the way I can. If they did, I'd be out of a job. But although I can do that well, there are many things I can't do at all. I've found that the more time I commit to becoming a good writer, the more my other talents diminish. I used to sew all my children's clothes. Now, I can hardly sew a straight line without getting stressed. It seems we all have certain levels of capability. When we try to do several things at the same level of performance, none of them will really stand out. When we focus on only one or two things, our capabilities become more evident. And how we divide our levels of capability among our talents is as individual as the talents themselves.

So, take a lesson from someone who had to learn the hard way. Don't be so focused on what you're *not* good at that you miss giving yourself an occasional pat on the back for what you *are* good at. And if you really pay attention, you might just discover that you're a lot more talented than you thought.

Stepping into the Dark

I began writing in earnest at the age of sixteen. It was something that felt good to me, and I made a conscious decision that I wanted to become a published novelist. If I had known how hard it would be, or how long it would take, I might have reconsidered. Of course, now that I've come to this point in my life, I'm grateful for the paths that got me here. In the middle of many ongoing struggles, it was difficult for me to see what was actually taking place. But I've learned that it's often only in retrospect that we come to understand the nature of a particular trial, and therefore glean its truest value.

I have come to believe that life is a series of long, dark tunnels. Typically we, as human beings, struggle along, trying to do the best we can with what we have to work with, and we spend a lot of time pressing forward toward the memory of some glimmer of light, with the hope that there will be more. We are occasionally blessed with spiritual experiences that keep us rooted in what we're doing and why. But in between those moments of light, we must endure the long dark tunnels.

If I had been able to look through the series of tunnels to see myself today, it would have been easy for me to keep writing and trying to sell my work. Today I can walk into an LDS bookstore and often see multiple shelves of books with my name on them. I have found a measure of success and it feels good. But for the many years I was struggling to get where I am, I had no idea how all of my efforts might turn out.

Writing novels is not like going to school to become a teacher, or a nurse, or an attorney. People respect that kind of education, and for the most part, you're guaranteed an income at the end of the path that will compensate for the time and money you've invested in your education. But it's not like that with creative professions. Even someone who achieves a degree in music is not guaranteed a successful career as an acclaimed musician. I prayerfully made the decision to *not* go to college. I'm not saying that I would endorse such a decision for someone else. I put a high value on education. I'm saying that it wasn't right for *me*, and I came to that decision through the guidance of the Spirit.

I came by my education in a more abstract way. But while I was trying to teach myself to become a better writer, I ran into many obstacles along the way. I actually went through a period of some years where I was *hiding*—a term I've taken from the parable of the talents found in the New Testament. I didn't know at the time that I was hiding. I figured it out much later, after I'd come out of hiding. Once again, I learned the lesson in retrospect.

We are all familiar with the parable of the talents. Those who took their talents and invested them and allowed them to grow were blessed with more talents. But the one who was given one talent took it and hid it because he was afraid. Subsequently, that talent was taken away from him and he was brought under condemnation. Hiding. Afraid. That was me. But allow me to explain why.

First of all, when you create something that is a part of you, it feels similar to having a baby. And when that something is judged and criticized, it's like having someone tell you your baby is ugly and stupid. So, after a large number of rejection letters in regard to my work, I was beginning to feel that, not only was my writing ugly and stupid, but I had to be crazy for ever thinking otherwise.

Secondly, I had trouble with feeling accepted. It's like this: when you move into a new neighborhood, women meet you at church, at the school, or they stop by to welcome you. You get into conversation, and inevitably they ask, "So, what do you do?"

If I had answered that question with any of at least a hundred possibilities, such as . . . *Oh, I do cross stitch, interior design, gourmet cooking, cake decorating, crafts, tole painting, scrap-booking, sewing, etc. etc.* . . . I would have received a response something like . . . *Oh, that's great!* Or . . . *We could do it together.* Or . . . *You could teach me.* Or . . . *Maybe you could do a mini-class at Relief Society.* But, no! I had to say, "I write romance novels." And the response was usually a polite, "Oh!" Followed by the dubious question, "And what do you *do* with these romance novels?" And I would say, "Well, I send them to publishing companies and they send me back nasty letters. It's great fun." And, to this day, I have never heard of a mini-class on writing romance novels.

Consequently, all things considered, I went into hiding. I tried all of those activities listed above and many others. Some I enjoyed. Some I could do adequately. Others I failed at miserably. But it was all part of a hiding process that I was stumbling through in the dark.

Then one day I woke up and realized that something inside of me was dying. Something very real and innately a part of me was shriveling up from lack of nourishment and sunlight. I didn't fully understand what it was and what it meant, but I did know that a novel had been swirling around in my head for more than three years, and it hadn't gone away in spite of all my efforts to hide. So, I wrote it. And I felt myself coming back to life. This was my first lesson in the need to fill and feed myself as a woman. I could be filled by writing. I found that when I took the time to write, I could be a better wife and mother, do my church job better . . . you get the idea. At that point, I had a long way to go in reaching the goals that I had set out to achieve, but at least I was pressing forward through those long, dark tunnels, instead of sitting still in the middle of one of them, too scared to move.

Years beyond that experience, I was deeply touched by a quote from President Harold B. Lee. "Walk to the edge of the light, and perhaps a few steps into the darkness, and you will find that the light will appear and move ahead of you."[1]

That's what I did. I stepped into the dark, and somehow managed to keep going. That's what we all have to do. We all have something we want to achieve, something that calls to us. And as long as we're genuinely trying to do what's right and press forward, eventually the light will come to show us the way. You don't have to know the ending. You just need faith enough to begin.

---

1. President Harold B. Lee as quoted by Boyd K. Packer, in Lucile C. Tate, *Boyd K. Packer: A Watchman on the Tower* (1995), 138.

Snowed Under

꧁꧂

There were many times through my years of struggling to make it as a writer that I came very close to giving up. I didn't necessarily *want* to quit writing. I think I just wanted to have what I was doing make sense. I'd spent years writing, putting in hours equivalent to a full-time job, with no compensation. No one actually came out and said, "When are you going to get the idea that you really don't have what it takes to make it as a writer?" But I felt it. How do you explain to people, even those closest to you, why you keep doing something that has absolutely no tangible result?

On top of that, the hours I spent writing were a definite strain on my time—more often than not. I always tried to keep church and family first, and always tried to keep my priorities straight. But having one story after another swirling through my head began to feel more like a curse than a blessing. I didn't *want* to quit writing, but I *did* want to uncomplicate my life. I wanted the stories to go away and leave me in peace if they weren't going to come to anything good. I wanted to be *normal.*

There were a number of times when I reached a breaking point. My solution was always to fast and pray. Perhaps I expected to be told that everything I'd written up to that point had been for some abstract purpose of teaching me patience, or that another season in my life would be better and that perhaps I should put off writing any more until my children were grown. Each time I went to the Lord in fasting and prayer, I got my answer. It didn't come quickly. It didn't come easily. But it always came. I knew I had to keep going. I didn't know why, and I couldn't fathom how all of it could possibly add up to something of value. But I forged ahead.

I want to share with you one experience in particular, because it taught me a valuable lesson regarding prayer and the promptings of the Spirit. I was at a particularly low time in my life. We were living in a 900-square-foot house, with four children, the youngest being two and three. If you can't easily visualize square footage, it was *very small*. My husband had been in the flooring business for many years, and had become a well-qualified installer. But because he was self-employed, we hadn't had any medical insurance for many years. We'd had two babies without insurance, and then my husband had an emergency gallbladder surgery. We were very blessed in being able to manage through all of that. Then my husband had a severe back injury that put him down flat for more than six weeks. Not only was he unable to work, he was told that he would never be physically capable of doing flooring again. So, once he *did* recover, he would be unemployed with no compensation. The ribbon on this package is that I was Young Women's president. Although the calling put a lot of demands and challenges on me, it also brought many blessings that got me through this difficult time. I was serving in this calling when I sold my first book.

While my husband was on a mattress on the living-room floor, and I was trying to deal with the strain of our finances, care for him, the home, and the children, as well as see to my Church responsibilities, we had one of the worst series of snowstorms I've seen in my adult life. For a couple of weeks, I couldn't go anywhere without digging out the car. And in the midst of all this, I had a story running around in my head like a hyperactive toddler demanding to be noticed. I wanted it to go away and leave me in peace. I didn't know how I could keep doing something so ridiculous in the face of life's challenges. I had begun to believe that I couldn't be a good writer *and* a good mother, so I had to give up one or the other. I couldn't give up my children. The answer seemed obvious.

I took the problem to the Lord. In the midst of my fasting and prayer, I went to sacrament meeting and entered the chapel to notice a woman across the room. She was divorced with grown children, so she lived alone. She and I were vaguely acquainted. The thought came into my mind that I should go and visit her. It wasn't a lightning bolt, or a burning in the bosom. It was just a simple thought that appeared and was quickly gone. After church I fed my family, made a quick batch of cookies, and took a plate of them to this woman's door. She invited me into her tiny front room. (All the houses in that ward were *very small.*) I had forgotten until then that this woman was an artist. I'd been in her home once before as a Relief Society counselor, but it had been a long time. Now I was overcome with the beauty of this woman's talent in the paintings that hung on her walls. We sat down to visit and quickly began discussing our shared creativity. She told me of the years she had painted with an easel in the kitchen and children playing around her feet. The conversation quickly became comfortable, and I quite naturally came around to admitting to my feelings. I told her I didn't think I could keep going, that it was probably ridiculous, that I couldn't do it all.

And then this sweet sister took my hand into hers, looked into my eyes and said, "Don't you ever, ever, ever give up on that creative part of you. Motherhood is important, yes, but it's only a brief span in your mortality. This is *you.* This is the thread that runs from your premortal existence to your postmortal existence. This will teach your children to respect you as a woman, not just an open purse and an open pantry."

How clearly I remember seeing the tears in her eyes just before I felt them come into mine. And then I felt a warmth penetrate me so fully, and so richly, that there was no denying the source of what I was feeling. I knew. I *knew* beyond any doubt that this woman had temporarily become an angel. She had become the mouthpiece for our Father in Heaven, to speak His words on my behalf. I received the answer to my prayers, and I came away from her home replenished, rejuvenated, and determined to keep going in the face of anything that might arise.

The lesson came for me much later when I pondered over that experience and asked myself some thought-provoking questions. What if I had rationalized away that simple prompting with the excuses of my situation? I'm too stressed, too discouraged, too busy. Let someone else take her cookies. What if I had brushed away the prompting with the belief that it was simply my imagination or a silly notion? How tragic it would have been!

I know now that this prompting from the Spirit was not to answer *her* prayers. It was to answer *mine.* I'm certain she appreciated the visit, but I wonder if she has any idea of the impact she had on me by being in tune enough to help answer my prayer. If I had ignored that prompting or brushed it aside, I wonder how long it might have been before my prayer would have been answered, if ever. I believe that our Father in Heaven is merciful, and He would have given me another chance, but I wonder how many more trials I might have had to endure if I had not been sensitive to the Spirit.

So, remember: when the going gets tough, we really can keep going . . . but *we* don't necessarily have to be tough. We just have to remember that we're not going it alone.

My Letter P Is Missing

When my son, John—now twenty—was about a year old, my husband bought a computer. Think for just a minute about how far computer technology has come in nineteen years. Even if you don't do a lot with computers, you must have a vague idea of the tremendous progress in the business. I've come up with a little analogy that might help. Imagine a wheeled cart. Imagine a Ferrari. Now imagine advancing from the technology of one to the other in nineteen years. That about covers it.

The computer I'm writing this book on is a laptop. It has several novels in it, folds up to less than two inches thick, and I can pick it up and take it to the dentist's office to work while I wait for the kids' check-ups. The computer we bought nineteen years ago was big, slow, ugly, and I *loved* it. Of course, I didn't know any better. I wrote and wrote and wrote on that computer. I think I wrote about twelve novels, all about the length of *Gone with the Wind,* and did a number of revisions on them. Let me repeat—I loved my computer. But one day it stopped working. One of the disk drives wouldn't run, which made it useless, since it didn't have a hard drive. I got down on my knees and explained the situation to my Father in Heaven. I reminded Him that we didn't have the money to repair this computer, let alone to buy a new one. I reminded Him that I had used this computer to write a road show and a couple of Relief Society skits, do Young Women's business, and write a ward newsletter. And I added, by way of apology, that I was writing a book.

I realize looking back (that's 20/20 hindsight) that I actually felt guilty for writing, because I enjoyed it. And I was actually *apologizing* to my Father in Heaven for using the gift He had given me. I know now that I was not nearly ready to succeed with my work, because I've come to believe that it's impossible to truly succeed at something when you don't understand its source or its purpose. However, I did have a lot faith . . . .

So I said my prayer, sat on my chair, and pushed the reset button. And the computer worked. In fact, it worked for another month or so. We actually developed a bit of a pattern. A prayer was good for four to six weeks. Then one day it finally wouldn't work any more at all. At this point I discovered that through the growth of technology, while I'd been mentally lost in other centuries, my computer had become obsolete. The company had gone under. The parts were not available. And (this is the really great part) the computer language, CPM, that all of my work was written in on those little floppy disks, had also become obsolete. Because my printer had been a lemon, only about ten percent of my work had been printed out. The rest was stuck on disks, written in a computer language that could not be read by an IBM computer without a working CPM computer—which didn't exist because it had become obsolete. *Discouragement.*

Amazingly, I came across a computer owned by a friend of a friend, *exactly* like mine. And she had used it for *recipes.* I'd written *Gone With the Wind* twelve times, and she'd used it for *recipes.* I figured if my computer figuratively had 200,000 miles on it, this one only had 5,000. The parts were interchangeable, and I had a friend who was willing to do the repairs out of the goodness of his heart. That all sounds great, right? Well, within just a few weeks, the same part failed on this computer. *The same part!* This should be a testament to how long the Lord kept my computer running. At the time it was extremely difficult. When the computer failed, it took two chapters with it, chapters for which I had no notes; no hard copy. I felt like my arm had been cut off. *Devastation.*

Surprisingly enough, this was about the time I decided to start writing LDS novels. Interesting, don't you think? I suddenly had overwhelming feelings about embarking on a project that I knew was inspired. And I had nothing to write with. I thought this was a strange phenomenon until it occurred to me that this pattern is typical in the scriptures. It's common for the Lord to ask a prophet to do something, such as. . . "Moses, free my people!" And the response is typically something like, "How and with what?" I had a great story idea, and I was basically wondering, *How and with what?* Margaret Mitchell wrote *Gone With the Wind* on a manual typewriter. Shakespeare used a quill. And of course, Mormon abridged all those records with . . . whatever it was he used to write on those gold plates.

Well, my husband bought a typewriter at Deseret Industries for eight or nine dollars. (I put it that way because I thought it was eight; he says it was nine. If I say eight or nine dollars, that is a metaphor for the compromise of marriage.) He bought it to use twice a year to put names on certificates for a community educa- tion class he taught. But I quickly took it over, and I started writing LDS novels. I know this is the timing because I have proof. The proof comes from the fact that this typewriter quickly stopped typing the letter *P*. I wrote *First Love and Forever,* and *First Love, Second Chances,* and parts of *Now and Forever, By Love and Grace, Return to Love,* and all of *Gables Against the Sky* (which was no small endeavor), all without the letter *P*. I want you to understand that this wasn't going on for a couple of weeks here. I used that stupid (I mean wonderful) old typewriter for a very long time.

In the meantime, I did a lot of complaining, and a lot of strug- gling to get something better to write with. I borrowed my mother's typewriter so I could type up the first three chapters and a synopsis of that first book so I could try to sell it. Otherwise, it wouldn't have looked very *rofessional.* But the ribbons for her machine were expensive, and it wasn't a practical option. I broke it a couple of times and had to find a way to get it repaired. And do you know what it's like to go back to using white-out after you've done word processing?

My mother, bless her heart, offered to pay the rent on a word processor. I don't know if she believed in me or if she just wanted her typewriter back (likely a little of both), but she came through. A word processor was much slower than a computer, but it was better than no letter *P*. By this time I was losing the tails on the *G*s and the *Y*s, as well.

Using this word processor, I was putting together some mate- rials to send to Australia for research. I had it all perfect and ready to print when suddenly it was all gone. I couldn't believe it! I went over everything I'd done in my head several times. I had been so careful, but my material was gone. I called the nice man at the store where we had gotten the machine. At his suggestion we took the machine in and he traded it for a new one, just like it, still in the box. I took it home. I got to exactly the same point, and the same thing happened. I *knew* I hadn't done anything wrong. I *knew!* And I will never forget the moment I lifted my fingers off those keys, and the Spirit spoke to my mind: *this is opposition.* I believe the Lord knew by then that if I didn't get a little light and understanding, I'd be doing something criminal with that piece of equipment. But even so, I felt so beaten down that the lesson He was trying to teach me didn't really penetrate. Adding to that, *First Love and Forever* had just been rejected—again! *Despair.*

I took the machine back. I didn't want another one. I felt jinxed. I felt like there was something wrong with me; that I was doomed to fail. I began questioning my sanity, my ability to feel the Spirit, to know the answers to prayers. Because I *had* been praying. I had prayed through all of this time that I would be able to buy another computer, so that I could have something to write with that I could depend on. And that's when I read the story in the book of Mosiah, chapter twenty-four. The people were in bondage. They poured out their hearts to the Lord. It says in verse fifteen, "Yea, the Lord did strengthen them that they could bear up their burdens with ease, and they did submit cheerfully and with patience to all the will of the Lord."

I was in bondage. But I was not submitting cheerfully and with patience. I was complaining. So, I stopped complaining. And through a series of little miracles, I was led to a *good* typewriter. It wasn't a computer, but it *did* type a beautiful letter *P.* So, I kept working, kept praying, and I told anyone who cared to listen that I was praying for a computer. But I didn't complain. Big difference. And not so many weeks later, the miracle occurred.

A missionary companion of my husband's was traveling through Utah from North Carolina. He stopped with his family for a brief visit. We covered all the usual topics of conversation, which included, of course, that I was computer challenged— meaning I didn't have one. Two weeks later, he called from North Carolina to tell me that he was getting a new computer, and he wanted to give me the old one. I bit my tongue so I wouldn't ask him what was wrong with it (jinxed as I was). He promptly shipped it to us, and wouldn't allow us to reimburse him for the shipping—which was good, because we couldn't have afforded it. Along with that computer came a letter, but before I tell you what it said, I have to tell you what else happened. Within a span of two weeks I was given this computer (which was in excellent working condition; it wasn't state of the art, but for word processing, it didn't have to be) as well as boxes of formatted disks, the word-processing software I had learned on my old computer (except that this was IBM compatible), and a table to put the computer on (no more working at the kitchen table). I was also given the (drum roll) just-released, state-of-the-art, software to transfer CPM to IBM on an IBM computer, so that all of my old work could be accessed. All in two weeks. All for a total of ten dollars.

Now, the letter that came with the computer: This dear friend told me the date he'd purchased the computer, and that he'd known it would only be temporary. He knew that when the time came, he would just find the right person to give it to. He told me that both he and his wife knew this computer was meant to be mine, and that the Lord had had me in mind right from the beginning. The date he bought it was before I'd ever had trouble with my original computer. The Lord had had me in mind all along.

I looked at my computer and I knew that what he'd said was true. I cried. And I got a little scared. This was not simply an answer to prayers. This was a miracle. It was as if the Red Sea had parted, and my computer had come through on dry ground. I knew then that my Heavenly Father actually *wanted* me to write. And it was up to me to find out what, and how He wanted me to go about it.

Occasionally I have to stop and tell myself that story again. It shows me the typical, but certainly not easy, process of refinement that seems necessary to accomplish any goal in this life that is truly worthwhile. I can see the patterns of testing. Would I stick it out? Keep going in spite of the discouragement, devastation, and despair? I learned that it really is true: the miracle comes *after* the trial of our faith.

The "Red Sea" computer has long ago been retired. I found it interesting that when I reached a point where I could afford to buy a computer, I was struck with an overwhelming feeling that I needed to do it *now.* I was able to transfer all of my work without any difficulty. Even though I always back everything up on multiple copies, unloading a hard drive before it crashes is much easier and less stressful than having to recover data after a crash. My son used the old computer for quite some time before it finally gave out. It never gave me a bit of trouble.

Now, not so many years later, I am sitting in a room with three computers. I use them for different things, and I often have all three going at the same time. I am grateful beyond words for the technology that allows me to write much faster and more efficiently than the prophet Mormon, or Shakespeare, or even Margaret Mitchell. And I am even more grateful for a merciful Father in Heaven who does, indeed, answer prayers.

A Matter of Perspective

——◦◦◦——

At the age of sixteen, I started writing romantic historical novels, and trying to sell them on the national market. For any of you who have read such books, well . . . shame on you. What I mean is . . . it's pretty difficult to find one that isn't disgusting. I confess that I read a few here and there, many years ago. But I quickly realized that what I was writing would never fit into the mishmash of worldly babble. Still, I kept trying to sell what I was writing. I'd send it to New York. I'd get a rejection letter. I did it again, over and over, somehow managing to get past the discouragement, the frustration, and the opposition; to press forward blindly through one dark tunnel after another.

Occasionally, in the midst of collecting rejection letters, someone would say to me, "Why don't you write an LDS novel? Maybe you should write for the Church market." And I would always say, "Nah, it's not my niche." Looking back at my firm determination on that count, I find it rather humorous—considering my success as an *LDS* romance author. I can easily imagine my Father in Heaven getting a good chuckle out of my insistence. He knew what I didn't know at the time. He knew that there were paths ahead for me that were better than the ones I'd chosen for myself. The Lord had a detour in mind for me that I hadn't yet caught sight of at that point in my life.

So, I kept writing new stories, kept sending them out, kept getting rejections. Then in September of 1991, I was at a League of Utah Writers' conference at a hotel in Provo, Utah. Between workshops, I overheard some women talking in the lobby about LDS romance novels. I'd never actually read one, so I was naturally surprised when I heard one of them say, "Oh, my gosh. They are so tacky. There's only one possible plot. One's a member of the

Church. The other isn't. The one that isn't joins the Church. They get married in the temple and live happily ever after."

I said nothing, but something inside of me felt very defensive. I thought, *There are all kinds of possible plots. You think because we're Mormons, we only have one story line to our lives?*

After these women moved away, a gentleman—who had overheard the same conversation—said to me, "Well, Anita, why don't you write an LDS romance? We'd publish it." He just happened to work for a prominent LDS publishing company. But you must understand that we were only vaguely acquainted. He had no idea what kind of writer I was. I truly believe that the Spirit kicked those words out of his mouth, and that night he probably got into bed and thought with horror, *What did I say?* But apparently he said the right thing, because my response to him was, "Well, maybe I will!"

During the next workshop, my mind began to spin. I pondered an idea that had been floating around in my mind for months with no apparent place to fit in with anything else I'd been writing. And I asked myself, *Could that be the premise for an LDS novel?* The answer was blatantly, "Yes!" By the time I went to bed that night, I had the plot for *First Love and Forever* worked out in my head.

I quickly set to work on the book (writing it without the letter *P*, if you'll recall), and I started doing some research on the LDS romance market. I went to several LDS bookstores, searching out novels that could give me some point of reference for what was currently selling. I was surprised to realize that I couldn't find any. There were less than a handful of LDS novels that had some minor level of *romance* in them, but there was no line of romances I had overheard those women talking about.

I started talking to women I knew loved to read—and I knew a lot of them. I came upon another startling discovery as I told them each in turn, "Guess what? I'm writing an LDS romance." Nine times out of ten, I got a response something like this: "Oh my gosh. Not one of those tacky books where one's a member and one's not. The one that's not joins the Church. They get married in the temple and live happily ever after."

I was flabbergasted! But as I pressed these same women with questions, I began to understand; the pieces of the puzzle began to fall into place. I heard over and over of how these women had once loved reading "LDS romances," but had reached a point where they became discouraged with what they were reading and had put them aside. Why? They told me life had been portrayed very idealistically. They came away from reading the stories feeling inadequate and frustrated. Their comments were all the same. "If this is how my life should be as a Mormon woman, then I can't measure up." Women quit reading them. Publishers quit publishing them.

Let me clarify an important point. Many of the books these women were talking about were actually quite good. I heard many compliments about certain stories and authors. Even though I had never read any of them, I have a deep respect for some of the authors of such books. They very much paved the way for what's taking place in the LDS fiction market today. The problem came in living in a world that was changing too quickly. Struggles of life were becoming more prominent. Reality was biting too hard and too fast.

Putting all of this information together, I determined that I was going to write an LDS novel unlike anything that had ever hit the market before. I was going to write books about realistic people, with realistic problems and weaknesses, who came to terms with their challenges through gospel principles. I started getting all kinds of ideas for LDS novels. It occurred to me that I could actually pioneer new ground in LDS fiction.

So I put together the first three chapters of that first book, along with a great synopsis, and a cover letter briefly explaining my other ideas. I sent them all to that acquaintance of mine at that publishing company, the first week of November. On December 23rd I received a rejection letter.

I regrouped and sent the book to another prominent LDS publishing company. They rejected it. Soon afterward I heard the managing editor of Covenant Communications speak at a seminar. As she went over the specifics of what they were looking for, I felt all warm and tingly inside. I *knew* they were my publisher. I just knew it. I promptly sent the book to Covenant. Their rejection was accompanied by pages and pages of criticism telling me how inadequate my book was.

By now I was an expert at getting rejected. I knew about the unspoken taboo against writing back to an editor once you'd been rejected. But I had a feeling that I should, anyway. I prayed about it, and I wrote a very careful letter to the editor, pointing out some conflicting comments I'd received in reference to my book. She wrote me back a very kind letter, telling me that she would be leaving Covenant. She invited me to address the criticisms I felt were valid and resubmit the book to the new managing editor. Well, that's fine. But I was angry, discouraged, and pretty upset.

In order to fully appreciate how upset I was, recall the long string of difficulties I'd also been having with my equipment. You also have to understand that the three publishers that had rejected my book were *the* three LDS publishers. There were several others in business, and some of them have come a long way in the past few years. But at the time most of them hadn't been in business long enough to make me feel comfortable with trusting them to successfully publish my book. I sent the book to a couple of them out of desperation anyway. One of them promptly rejected it. The other one finally sent me a rejection letter about two years after the book had been published. It was in its fifth printing and had won some awards, but they told me that it "did not suit their editorial needs." Now, that certainly puts perspective on rejection.

However, when you're in the midst of it, rejection can be devastating—especially when it's happened so many times. Emotionally I was stretched to my limits on the matter. But given some time, some prayer, and the perspective that comes with both, I dusted myself off and found the strength to go back and do as that editor had suggested. I pulled out that LDS book I'd been trying to sell, and the many pages of criticism that had come along with Covenant's rejection. I went through the book carefully, analyzing every little point that had been criticized. I took advantage of two people I trusted very much—a close friend and my sister—who both knew the book very well. They were also very honest. I knew that neither of them would tell me something was good if it wasn't. Following this long, grueling process, I made the decision to leave the book exactly as it had been. Remember, the editor had asked me to fix what I felt was valid. Well, in my heart I didn't feel that *any* of what had been said was valid. Without changing a single word, I resubmitted the book exactly as I had submitted it the first time.

Covenant offered me a contract. They asked for no revisions on the book beyond the usual line editing. They made it the lead fiction title in their fall 1994 line, and it became an immediate bestseller. Ironically, this particular book won the Best Fiction Award from the Independent LDS Booksellers—an award that had never before been given to a Covenant book.

After that award was given publicly, the editor who had originally suggested I write an LDS novel approached me and adamantly declared, "I never saw this book." We had a pleasant conversation over the quirks and challenges of the publishing business, most specifically how good books occasionally slip through the slush pile of submissions unnoticed. From my perspective, I firmly believe that my work had a time and a place to come forth. And until the circumstances were right, it just didn't get into the right hands, specifically the hands of someone who could read it and catch the vision of what I was attempting to accomplish.

In 1997, when the Church was celebrating the sesquicentennial of the pioneers' arrival in Utah, Covenant presented me with a special award for pioneering new ground in LDS fiction. I recalled, years earlier, that very idea being in my mind. The idea had become crushed beneath the rejection and discouragement, but I believe now that the Spirit put that idea into my mind, if only to give me a momentary glimpse of my potential.

I know most people will never face the literal rejection of trying to get an artistic invention recognized. But every one of us will likely face some form of rejection in this life. It's all part of the trial and growth of the human experience. It could be facing unemployment with repeated job possibilities falling through. It could be a desire to marry and have a family but seeing every available suitor turn away. And I'm certain that in some cases the perspective won't fully come into place on this side of the veil. But if I had known then what I know now, I could have spared myself a great deal of anxiety and grief. What I know now is this: God was always in charge. Even at my lowest moments, when everything seemed bleak and hopeless, He knew that it was all part of the plan He'd had in mind right from the start. He knew the necessary steps and the mandatory growth that had to take place for the puzzle pieces to come together.

If I had it to do over again, I would change only one thing. I would do my best to trust in God and not allow discouragement to overtake me. I prayed about every step I took, and I kept taking them. But the perspective of hindsight has made it clear to me that I didn't have to drive and navigate at the same time. I just had to keep my hands on the wheel and keep going. The Great Navigator took care of the rest.

Never Give Up

———∽∽∽———

I have borrowed the title for this chapter from a conference address I heard given in 1987 by Elder Joseph B. Wirthlin. It came at a time, not unlike many other times before and since, when I felt tempted to let go of my dream and throw in the towel. But this particular conference address seemed to be written just for me and my sister; we were both struggling along with our different writing projects at the time, and were encountering a great deal of discouragement. Phrases from that address have hovered in my mind all these years, prompting me to press forward in many matters, both spiritual and temporal, when I felt tempted to quit.

Whatever you might be struggling to achieve at this time in your life, I highly recommend that you read this particular address, which will save me from having to quote the entire thing. However, allow me to share a couple of my favorite tidbits.

Perseverance is a positive, active characteristic. It is not idly, passively waiting and hoping for some good thing to happen. It gives us hope by helping us realize that the righteous suffer no failure except in giving up and no longer trying. When some people have a difficult job to do, they give up everything else until that job is finished. Others just give up.[1]

Elder Wirthlin goes on to share the quote: *The line between failure and success is so fine that we are often on the line and do not know it. How many a man has thrown up his hands at a time when a little more effort, a little more patience, would have achieved success?*[2]

At the time, I wondered if I was actually standing on the line and just needed to keep going a little further. It was actually several years before I moved to the other side of that line, but there were many times when I told myself, "You're standing on the line, Anita. Just hang on a little longer."

The greatest message I absorbed from Elder Wirthlin's words came from his sharing a story about Winston Churchill. After reiterating what a great man Winston Churchill was, Elder Wirthlin tells of the prime minister's speaking at a school he'd attended as a boy. The headmaster told the students that they had better be prepared with their notebooks to write down what Mr. Churchill would say, and to remember it all of their lives. He got up and said, "Never, never, never give up."[3] Then he sat down.

That's what I want to tell you now. Whether you're praying for a difficult child to come around, struggling to achieve success in a career, an education, or at home, or you're focused on any other number of eternal goals, remember to never, never, never give up. One way or another, there is light on the other side of that tunnel. I recall hearing a song many years ago by the English band Level 42, called "Standing in the Light." I was unable to find its origin or any specific information on the song, but I recall its message well. The song was about a genius child who never fit in, but one day became great. More recently I came across another song that used the same phrase. *Holding on, now I'm standing in the light. Now I'm glad I kept holding on, now I'm glad I had soul enough.*[4]

Even though I have achieved many goals, and I have seen some level of fruition of my dream, I know in my heart that there are many steps left to take. I know now that achieving success is not a destination, but a lifelong process, and that the ultimate success is standing in the light of our Father in Heaven as we return to live in His presence. We just have to keep holding on, and never, never, never give up.

1. Elder Joseph B. Wirthlin, "Never Give Up," *Ensign,* November 1987.

2. *Ibid.*, quoting from *Second Encyclopedia,* ed. Jacob M. Brand (Englewood Cliffs, N.J.: Prentice Hall, 1957) 152, author unknown.

3. *Ibid.*, quoting Winston Churchill, from "These Are Great Days," in *War Speeches,* ed. Charles Eada (Boston: Little Brown and Co, 1942) 286-88.

4. Steve Winwood and Will Jennings, "Holding On," from the Steve Winwood album, *Roll With It,* 1988.

The Whisperings of Destiny

I finally got a book contract sixteen years—to the month—from when I had started writing at the age of sixteen. After spending half my life trying to achieve a goal, and suddenly achieving it, I found myself a little disoriented. Getting a book published didn't bring drastic changes into my life. I hadn't expected it to. I'd always known where my priorities and values were. I'd always committed myself to putting church and family first. I had accepted years earlier that, in spite of how important my writing was to me, I could never expect it to make me happy. I knew that if I could be happy as an unpublished writer, I would be happy as a published one.

However, I did find myself doing a great deal of soul searching. Looking back over the experiences that had led me to the achievement of this goal, I was amazed—and even a bit confused—as I tried to comprehend the full spectrum of all that had taken place. While I was in this state of being somewhat dazed over the forthcoming publication of my first book, my dear friend Ellen approached the final stages of her life, due to her long-time battle with cancer. She spent the final weeks of her life at her parents' home in Spring City, Utah, more than an hour's drive from where I was living in Orem. One day a week, along with three other friends, I went to Spring City to visit Ellen. We had great visits, with lots of laughter and conversation.

On a particular day in May, we knew it would be the last time. Ellen was mostly incoherent while we were there. We all said our good-byes the best we could, and on the way home everyone was more or less silent. It was clearly evident to all of us that we had just shared a profound experience, with the veil being extremely thin as Ellen prepared to pass through it.

Through the next couple of days, that spiritual sensation hovered close to me. I felt prone to tears, even though I was relatively numb in regard to Ellen's death. I sensed somehow that the Spirit was trying to teach me something, but I was wandering around in a fog with no idea what that *something* might be.

Two days after my visit with Ellen, I turned to my patriarchal blessing, specifically searching for an answer to all that I was feeling. As I read a particular sentence that I had read dozens of times before with no impact, it suddenly made such profound sense that it took my breath away. Only a heartbeat later, I was overcome with one of the most significant spiritual experiences of my life. I learned later that such an experience had been defined by Joseph Smith as *quickening*, when the Spirit teaches something instantly that would otherwise take hours or even days to learn.

An enormous perspective opened up in my mind. I understood in that moment that I had been a storyteller in my premortal existence. I had been given this gift by my Father in Heaven, with a specific purpose and mission attached to it. I clearly understood the paths my life had taken—the financial struggles, the personal struggles, the strain in seemingly every aspect of my life. It had all been for the purpose of strengthening and preparing me for the mission I was about to embark upon as my first book was being prepared to come into the world. I understood the opposition I had been subjected to, and how hard Satan had been working to hold me back from accomplishing my mission. I also understood that the opposition had not ended; in fact, it had only begun. I knew in that moment that my stories could change lives for the better. And while I had always written with a married-woman audience in mind, I knew in that moment that I would touch the lives of people of all ages, both men and women.

In the years since, I have seen the manifestation of what I learned in that moment. I have received hundreds and hundreds of letters from people—young and old, male and female—expressing gratitude for the stories that have helped them through their struggles, validated their feelings, and encouraged changes in their lives. I have met even more people who have expressed similar thoughts in person. While I cannot describe the personal fulfillment of such a response to my work, it is also very humbling. I must give credit where credit is due. In spite of the time it took me to fully come to terms with my gift and its source and purpose, I think I always instinctively knew there was a power greater than myself stirring these stories in me. As I have learned to more fully recognize the workings of the Spirit in my life, I have come to see that I have never been writing alone. There are times when I feel as if I'm just the typist.

Don't get the idea that my stories all come this way from beginning to end and all I do is type. It's more like I'm given bits and pieces that way, and I have to work very hard to fill in the rest. Nevertheless, I know the ingredient in these books that has the power to change lives for the better comes directly from the Spirit. I felt the full perspective of this when I was once struggling with a particular bout of writer's block. In my Book of Mormon study, I was reading about the brother of Jared, as he prepared to take the people across the water in the barges. Responding to his need to provide light in the barges, he took stones to the Lord and asked that He touch them with His finger to give them light. I likened that to the many years I have spent learning how to write well. (And I've worked very hard.) Figuratively, I know how to find the stones, and I know how to make them smooth. But until they are lit by the finger of God, they are nothing. To this day, I can be completely crippled in writing a story if inspiration isn't present to some degree. *I know from whence my blessings come.*

I once heard Michael McLean say that he didn't feel like he wrote the songs, he only got to hear them first. How deeply I related!

While I was pondering the paths my life had taken and all I had been given, I was reading Joseph Smith's account of the first vision. It's evident that in these scriptural accounts we're given, the writer only scratches the surface. I like to try and read between the lines, and imagine the full depth of what was really taking place. So I had to ask myself: why would a fourteen-year-old boy be so concerned and upset over the different religions available? I've had fourteen-year-old boys at my house, and it doesn't seem the typical psychology for a boy that age to be so preoccupied with religion. But Joseph Smith was.

I've wondered why, after reading in the book of James that he needed to pray in order to get his answer, he didn't just wait until everyone else was asleep and kneel down by his bed. Joseph Smith was a very busy young man with a lot of responsibilities. Why did he make so much effort to go so far away from the house and be completely alone?

We all know what happened when Joseph Smith uttered that prayer. And we know the resulting, incomparable impact on the world. We also know, because the scriptures tell us, that Joseph Smith was foreordained to be the prophet to usher in this dispensation. He had been trained for it, prepared, and taught before he was ever born. When he came to this earth, the veil was drawn over his mind, just as it is with each of us. But the veil was not drawn over his heart. It is through our hearts, or through our feelings, that the Spirit confirms his message to us. It is through our hearts that we stay in touch with the home we left before we came here. Joseph Smith listened to his feelings, and his feelings led him to his destiny.

As this perspective settled into my mind, I was able to relate in some small way to Joseph, and the understanding of my own situation deepened. Looking back through the years of my struggles to achieve my dream, the one thing that kept me going was that feeling somewhere deep inside that led me to believe there was some greater purpose, even if I didn't understand what it was. I followed my feelings, and my feelings led me to my destiny.

So, I would like to pose the question to you . . . do you know what gift your Father in Heaven gave *you* before you left his side? The scriptures tell us that each person is given at least one gift. Do you know what yours is? If you know what it is, do you use it? Do you use it to its full potential? Do you use it to make a difference? Are you hiding your candle under a bushel? Are you hiding your talent in the earth out of fear? Or are you so caught up in feelings of inadequacy that you're certain you couldn't possibly have a gift of any value?

Let's talk about gifts for a minute. We tend to look at gifts from a very worldly perspective. A gifted athlete. A gifted artist. A gifted musician. We tend to believe if you can't perform it on a stage or hang it on the wall, it isn't a gift.

Have you ever gone through the grocery checkout line of the *gifted* cashier? She's the one who so obviously loves her job that she adds a little something extra to her encounter with every customer.

She's the one you prefer working with, because there's something you can't quite pinpoint about her that makes the drudgery of grocery shopping almost bearable.

Have you ever considered the gift of friendship? The gift of compassion? The gift of teaching? The gift of listening? What about the gift of appreciating other people's gifts? Gifts are as unique and innumerable as we are. Gifts become evident through our Church callings, our occupations, and our relationships. Gifts come in different seasons of our lives. I've known many women who have discovered, once their children were grown, that they could finally think clearly enough to realize they had a gift. On the other hand, exploring our gifts through those child-rearing years can give our lives balance and teach our children to discover their own gifts. And I believe that some of the greatest gifts manifest themselves within the walls of our own homes.

So, I offer you a challenge: find your gifts. Listen to the compliments you receive. Listen to your feelings. Read your patriarchal blessing. Get down on your knees and ask your Heavenly Father to help you find your gift and use it according to His will. Ask Him to help you overcome the feelings and fears that hold you back, and then watch the magic unfold. But don't expect it to happen quickly or easily. I believe that the more intense the treasure hunt, the more valuable the treasure.

Imagine for a moment that the life you lived in the premortal existence is something like a black-and-white picture. When you come through the veil, that picture breaks into a thousand pieces, like a jigsaw puzzle. As you go through your life, following your feelings and listening to the Spirit, you find those pieces one by one. Occasionally you have an experience that suddenly connects one cluster to another. The further you get into your life, and the more effort that goes into putting the puzzle together, the more you come to understand who and what you really are. But as the puzzle comes together, it's now full color and three-dimensional. This is the picture that you take back to your Father in Heaven. This is the gift you give back to Him, as you say, "This is what I made of my life and the gifts You gave me."

So, find your gifts. Follow your dreams. And don't ever forget to give credit where credit is due.

PHOTO BY "PICTURE THIS . . . BY SARA STAKER"

About the Author

Anita Stansfield has been writing for more than twenty years, and her best-selling novels have captivated and moved hundreds of thousands of readers with their deeply romantic stories and focus on important contemporary issues. Her interest in creating romantic fiction began in high school, and her work has appeared in national publications. *Reflections* is her twentieth work to be published by Covenant.

Anita lives with her husband, Vince, and their five children and two cats in Alpine, Utah.